AN INQUIRY INTO SOCIALISM

AN INQUIRY INTO SOCIALISM

THOMAS KIRKUP

GYAN

Published by

Gyan Publishing House
5, Ansari Road
Daryaganj, New Delhi-110002
Phone: 011-47034999, 9811692060
E-mail: books@gyanbooks.com

Distribution Network
gyanbooks.com
India, USA, Canada, UK, Australia, France

ISBN: 978-81-212-8995-5 (PB)
First Published, 1887

2nd Impression 2023

Printed at: Gyan Press, Delhi.

AN INQUIRY INTO SOCIALISM
AUTHOR: THOMAS KIRKUP

AN INQUIRY INTO SOCIALISM

AN INQUIRY INTO SOCIALISM

BY

THOMAS KIRKUP

THIRD EDITION

REVISED AND ENLARGED

LONGMANS, GREEN, AND CO.
39 PATERNOSTER ROW, LONDON
NEW YORK, BOMBAY, AND CALCUTTA
1907

PREFACE

THIS book was first published at the end of 1887. It went into a second edition in 1888, and has been out of print since 1890.

For the present edition I have very carefully revised the book in the light of the fresh knowledge and experience which we have gained since 1888. But I have not found it necessary to alter it in any essential respect. The changes I have made are such as have been requisite to bring it up to date in its references to recent and contemporary events or desirable for the further clearing up and development of a great and perplexing subject.

As I stated in my preface to the first edition, 'the aim of this book is to bring out what is fundamental in Socialism, both as contrasted with the prevailing social system and with theories for which it is usually mistaken.' It is an attempt to discover what is enduring and beneficent in the socialist movement by a study of the forces, principles, and tendencies which are at work in the present stage of historic evolution. An inquiry into Socialism naturally divides itself into three parts. We must first consider the problem which Socialism undertakes to solve; and this leads us to study the origin and nature of the present system. We have next to determine as clearly as possible what Socialism is and the nature of the solution it offers. And, lastly, we have to discuss how far the solution is likely to be successful. These points I have treated in succession, but without adhering to a rigid division of topics.

The reader will find also that I have not adopted a formal and technical style of treatment. Socialism is not a technical subject merely, but a wide human question, most intimately connected with the moral, social, and political development of the present age. It appeals to the general intelligence. In such a movement the only effective teachers and critics are Time and his daughter Experience, who have indeed already taught us some very notable lessons. The good reader will find in this book the net result of an extensive and prolonged study of the socialist movement as illustrated by these two great instructors of erring men.

The 'Inquiry' is a companion volume to my 'History of Socialism.' Those who desire references to authorities, or who wish to study the development of socialistic theories, will find them there. But I should like here to make special acknowledgment of my obligations among German economists to Roscher, Adolf Wagner, Adolf Held, and, above all, to Schäffle; also to Laveleye and J. S. Mill.

T. KIRKUP.

CONTENTS

INQUIRY INTO SOCIALISM

CHAPTER I

INTRODUCTION

MEN now generally recognise that socialism is one of the most remarkable forces of the age in which we live, and that it is spreading in almost every part of the civilised world. It is a vague movement, the scope and meaning of which cannot easily be defined. And there are two very obvious reasons why this should be so ; we have not yet decided how to use the word, and the movement itself is in a state of incessant development. Both name and thing are to a very large degree unfixed.

For the present, however, we may say that socialism claims to be the economic and social side of a wider historical process, which in politics is democracy and in ethics means justice, humanity, and generous service to society ; a process which set in long ago, but whose accumulating effects are only beginning to be really felt. While it professes first of all to be a movement for the deliverance of the poor, the aim of socialism is towards the renovation and progress of the entire human society.

Socialism is therefore the outcome of forces which are vast, real, and incessantly growing, but have as yet only partially taken shape. The conditions which led to its rise and growth did not come into action till about the end of the eighteenth century. It is a modern movement. There is a reasonable historical use of the word, and in this reasonable sense socialism may be said to have a definite beginning with the theories of Robert Owen in England, and of Saint-Simon and Fourier in France.

The origin of a name which is now one of alarm and of hope throughout the civilised world is even more recent. It appears to have been first used in the 'Poor Man's Guardian' in 1833, and became current in England in 1835, during the agitation of Robert Owen.

From the first diffusion of the new creed its history has been a strangely chequered one. It has assumed many forms, and known a great variety of fortune, but on the whole it has followed a continuous line of development, and made vast progress. It was in 1817 that Robert Owen published his plans of social reconstruction. The theories of Saint-Simon began definitely to take a socialistic direction about the same time. The newest phase of the revolutionary spirit had its rise just two years after the Revolution had apparently received its quietus at Waterloo, and since then it has grown both in intensity and volume.

The history of the early socialism is at first sight one of absolute failure, the causes of which are only too manifest. With much that was valuable the early theorists mixed a large proportion of activity that was extravagant, Utopian, and subversive of social order.

But it would be a great mistake to estimate the pioneer movements of the world by their immediate and visible results. In the schools of Saint-Simon, Fourier, and Owen the seeds of fresh and vital thought regarding the first principles of society were liberally cast abroad. A rude shock was for a time at least given to the self-complacent optimism of an era which had no reason to be thus content with its achievements. Through the efforts of the early socialism not a few of the most gifted youth of France were inspired with a generous enthusiasm for human progress, which was afterwards displayed in many and various walks of life. J. S. Mill has narrated in his autobiography how the growth of his opinions was affected by the discussions of French socialism. In the days of its decline the agitation of Owen gave birth to what is called the co-operative movement, which has grown from the smallest beginnings to be a great and beneficent influence.

The gravest error of the early socialists lay in the fact that they associated their central principle with so much extraneous matter of an objectionable kind; and this mistake has been equalled by the perversity with which ordinary history has fixed attention on this matter, as if it were the very essence of socialist teaching. It might be thought that, while recording and condemning the errors of original thinkers, it should be one of the main functions of history to make prominent and perpetual whatever is salutary and suggestive of better things. With regard to the early socialism this reasonable method has been reversed. Of the valuable aspects of its teaching current history has had little or nothing to say, but it has persistently emphasised the quixotic and extravagant.

In the time which preceded the revolution of February 1848, Paris was the great centre of social fermentation, when new and startling theories for the reconstruction of society grew up rapidly. The school of Fourier had a brief period of prosperity. Cabet published his 'Voyage en Icarie' in 1840. Louis Blanc's 'Organisation du Travail' appeared in the same year. Proudhon's attack on property also came out in 1840, and was only the first of a series of trenchant and paradoxical utterances, calculated alike to shake orthodox economists and too sanguine socialistic dreamers out of their easy optimism. Paris was at this period the place of pilgrimage for the inquiring and revolutionary spirits of Europe. In the few years which preceded 1848 it was visited by three men who were destined to play a great *rôle* in the social revolution—by Lassalle, the founder of the Social Democracy of Germany, by Marx, the organising and directing head of the International, and the expounder of scientific socialism, and by Bakunin, the apostle of Anarchism. It was here, too, that Mr. Ludlow became acquainted with Fourierism, and thus learned those principles of association which were utilised in the Christian socialist movement in England.

The cause of the working man has perhaps never had such an opportunity as under the Provisional Government which ruled in France during the spring of 1848. Had Louis Blanc been an energetic leader, had he decisively appealed to the working classes of Paris and the industrial centres of France, socialism might have won at least a temporary triumph. But

Louis Blanc had not personal force and decision of character enough to fit him for such a career. He was an amiable and genial enthusiast, who was little qualified to be a leader and controller of men on a large scale. The opportunity was lost; but the national strength of France had to be put forth in order to suppress the rising of the discontented masses of Paris which afterwards ensued.

The Christian socialism of England, under the leadership of Maurice and Kingsley, did a good work in protesting against the evils of the competitive system, in insisting upon the necessity of ethical and spiritual principles as the saving elements of society, and in promoting co-operation; but for some years even the co-operative movement was not a very great success. About 1850 the socialist movement in France and England, which had run more or less on parallel lines since 1817, had come to a close.

In the period which followed the abortive efforts of the revolutionary year 1848, socialism was considered even by just and sympathetic students to be dead, without hope of resurrection. By such as took the trouble to think of it at all it was believed to be a transient social disease, a phase of revolutionary frenzy, which had troubled certain hot and fevered brains, but which had passed away, never to return. Yet even before the failures of 1848 the beginnings of a socialistic propaganda of a far more powerful and resolute character than anything previously known had already been made in a new quarter.

There were two European countries which were supposed to be proof against socialistic ideas, Germany and Russia. Neither of them had a proletariat in the modern sense of the word, and Russia especially was believed to have in its communal institutions a firm bulwark against discontent, and a guarantee that the mass of the people could not sink into the condition of poverty and demoralisation which characterised the workmen of the West. It was in those two countries that the subsequent development of socialism was destined to be most potent and virulent.

The revolutionary thinkers with whom German and Russian socialism originated had all made their first studies in the movement during the restless years which culminated in 1848. But their activity did not take a notable historic form till a later period.

Considered as a historical movement German socialism really began with the agitation of Lassalle in 1863. Since that time its career has been one of rapid and almost uninterrupted progress. When Lassalle began his propaganda in Berlin he could hardly obtain a hearing even from working-class audiences. At the first election for the Imperial Diet, in 1871, Social Democracy counted only 6,695 votes in the capital. For the whole Empire they polled only 102,000 votes and returned only two members. In 1877 their entire poll for the Empire had increased to nearly half a million. It declined during the period when the anti-socialist legislation was being discussed and passed, but it soon began to rise again. At the election of 1887 it was 763,000, while in Berlin alone it was 93,000, and in Hamburg 51,000. In 1890 the entire socialist poll rose to 1,427,000, in 1893 it was 1,786,000, and 2,100,000 in 1898. They won their greatest triumph in 1903, when they had 3,010,000 votes, or nearly one-third of the whole number cast in the Empire, and returned eighty-one members to the Reichstag. Even at the general election of 1907, when they returned only forty-three members, they polled about 3,250,000, being one million more than the next strongest party, the Centre. At the great centres of population, as in the Empire generally, they were now the strongest party.

This marvellous change has been produced in little more than a generation—that is to say, in the period which elapsed between 1871 and 1907. But we cannot rightly estimate the magnitude of the transformation without taking into account the influence which it has exercised on German thought. A movement which in England not many years ago was dismissed with an idle epigram or with an inexcusable perversion and misrepresentation of the truth has been deemed worthy of grave and judicial treatment by her best thinkers. It has found converts among her ablest economists, and where it has not commanded assent it has very powerfully altered the prevailing tone of thought and determined the direction of inquiry. Its influence in this way can fairly be compared to that of Darwinism in natural science. It has also seriously affected legislation. The cause of the poor man was with all sincerity and earnestness adopted by the first Emperor and his redoubtable Chancellor, and an important series of measures for the insurance of workmen against accident, sickness, and old age were passed. Bismarck was above all things a realist statesman, who had his eyes open to the facts and forces with which he had to deal. Even the strongest rulers must obey the dominant tendencies of their time. Bismarck established a new and a better order over a wide expanse of human affairs, and prepared the way for further progress.

In the course of its history the Social Democratic party of Germany has given abundant proof of intelligence, discipline, and enthusiasm. Since the world began no organisation of working men has had such a record. But its career has been marred by the ultra-revolutionary dogmatism of its beliefs and policy. The healthy and natural development of democracy in Germany has been obstructed and weakened by its excessive loyalty to the traditions of the Marx school. Its social task has in the same way been postponed or only very partially performed. It has not been true to its name and mission of Social Democracy. Without sufficient reason its leaders have at many points placed themselves in opposition to the national life and spirit of Germany, and accordingly they and the cause they represent have suffered. The first need of the German Social Democracy now is to emancipate itself from the traditions of the past, and to frame a programme and a policy suited to the circumstances in which it actually finds itself.

Lassalle was the originator of the Social Democracy of Germany, but he was in some measure indebted to Karl Marx for his scientific weapons; and by the influence of Marx it has been controlled chiefly since the founder's death. Beyond comparison Marx has done more than any other man to diffuse the socialistic creed. He was a man of strong personality, with a vast learning wielded by an intellect of marvellous acuteness and power. All these great gifts he devoted to the proletariat, whose cause he served for forty laborious years, both in agitation and in propaganda, and in scientifically working out the socialistic conception of social evolution. Besides so largely controlling the Social Democratic movement of Germany he was the real founder and chief of the International, which from 1864 to 1872 exercised no little influence in Europe, though its real power was by no means commensurate with the attention it excited.

A notable event in the development of socialism was the revolt of the Commune of Paris in 1871. The aims of that rising are probably not even yet quite clear. Perhaps they were not quite clear to the leaders themselves. But there can be no doubt it was a rising for the autonomy of Paris, which has always been far in advance of the provinces; and though the socialists formed only a small minority of its leading members, the movement was the outcome of a profound social discontent. It was a movement for home rule in Paris based on social discontent and supported by the masses of her population.

The revolutionary movement of Russia has taken an aggressive form suited to the political and other conditions of the country. The social movement of Russia did not properly begin till 1870; and at first its aim was by a peaceful propaganda among the people to prepare the way for a new order of things. But as this activity was repressed by the government without mercy, the revolutionary party also determined to show no mercy, and after 1878 they carried on an implacable war against the Czardom. It was a struggle against an autocratic rule conducted by a band of resolute men and women, well educated, imbued with the most advanced ideas of Western Europe, and wielding without reserve the resources of modern science. In 1881 the conflict had its catastrophe for the time being in the assassination of the Emperor Alexander II. Under his successor, Alexander III., the movement was suppressed. It began to gather head again before the end of the nineteenth century, and on the failure of Russia in the war with Japan it broke out with extraordinary intensity. The socialists have been the moving spirits in the terrible revolutionary risings against the Czardom.

Repressed for a time by the overthrow of the Commune in 1871, the social movement in France soon became active again. From 1876 the socialist parties have through a chequered experience of debate and dissension advanced both in numbers and organisation. At the general election of 1906 the socialist vote rose to 1,120,000, while seventy-five socialists and 143 radical socialists were returned to the Chamber. Socialism is making a like advance in Belgium, Austria, and Italy, in Holland and Denmark, and even in Norway and Sweden. It may generally be said that in the large towns and industrial centres of the Continent socialism, more or less conscious and avowed, and more or less revolutionary, is the real creed of the working men; and from time to time it certifies its strength by large meetings and demonstrations usually well disciplined and organised, but occasionally attended with disturbance.

Great Britain for a long time led the way in measures of practical socialism, such as factory Acts. Since 1883 we have had a revival of avowed and organised socialism, and the trade unions have been considerably leavened with socialist opinion and the socialist spirit. But it was not till the general election of 1906 that a Labour-Socialist party appeared as a conspicuous force in national affairs.

Those who attribute the growth of socialism merely to backward political conditions, and regard freedom as an effectual remedy for discontent, would do well to give a little attention to America. There we find signs of gathering social trouble and of the developing antagonism between labour and capital, which point to far deeper sources of evil. For many years America has been receiving from Eastern and Southern Europe a vast mass of immigrants, whom she cannot easily assimilate. All the best land is passing into private hands. Soon there will be no space for the further extension of homesteads. Before many years are over the wide regions of the West, which have so long afforded scope for the enterprise and relief for the discontent of the civilised world, will have been occupied. Land will no longer be obtainable at prices which the labourer can pay. It will be a turning-point in the history of the poor man. For obvious reasons connected with the marvellous extent and immense natural resources of the country and with the energetic character of the people, America has rapidly become the seat of the most gigantic industrialism in the world. The Republic is confronted with a colossal capitalism organised in trusts such as men have never before seen. And it has labour organisations which are to a large degree socialistic in aim and tendency. In America the problems of the old world are reappearing under new conditions determined by the special circumstances of the country.

Socialism in its more practical forms is rapidly

growing in the English colonies at the Antipodes, and even in South Africa. There is an active socialist party in Japan.

From the brief review which we have thus made of the external history of socialism we have seen how the theory of a few visionary and Utopian thinkers has become a great power in the world. The cause of labour, which it claims to represent, has twice been concerned with risings in Paris, which it required the exertion of the national strength of France to repress. It now confronts with unflinching resolution two of the strongest governments in the world, Germany and Russia. It is still growing in almost every country of Europe, and in many great countries beyond it. In a form purified from the Utopian and extravagant elements with which during its history it has so frequently been associated, it has gained the adherence of some of the greatest economic thinkers of recent times. This is a considerable record for a movement which has not been a century in existence.

To avoid repetition we have made no special reference to the nature of the theories advocated by the different socialists. These theories can be much more comprehensively stated in view of the general development of the subject, and accordingly we now proceed to give, in a preliminary way but in a connected form, the cardinal principle of socialism. What is fundamental in all the phases of socialism has been well expressed by the Saint-Simonian school. The key-note of the past has been the exploitation of man by man in the three forms of slavery, serfdom, and wage-labour. The key-note of the future must be the exploitation of the globe by man *associated* to man.

As slave-labour and serf-labour have been the prevalent forms in past ages of history; as wage-labour is the prevalent form at present; so for the future the prevalent form contemplated by socialism is associated or co-operative labour. Both on historical and theoretical grounds there can be no doubt that such is the essence of socialism. To prove it fully we should need to quote at large the literature of socialism. But it will suffice here to show that the different schools and phases of socialism are variations of this fundamental idea; varied by nearly every possible difference of modifying condition and circumstance, and mixed up with the most contradictory opinions in religion, philosophy, politics, and social ethics. In the historical development of socialism three phases may be broadly recognised.

The *first stage* was marked by private experiment in founding associations especially in connection with the schools of Owen and Fourier. Apart from many fantastic details which especially characterised the schemes of Fourier, these associations were intended to be self-supporting communities based on co-operative labour of the most varied kind, with the best available machinery and uniting all the advantages of town and country life. Most of them failed in the form given them by their founders, but they exercised an important influence on the subsequent development of socialism.

Of the *second stage* the most characteristic features are to be found in the proposals of Louis Blanc and Lassalle. The theories of Owen, Saint-Simon, and Fourier grew up under the reaction consequent on the excesses and conflicts of the French Revolution. By the time of Louis Blanc, however, the democratic development had resumed its natural course, and the socialist movement joined it. Louis Blanc and Lassalle advocated, *first*, a democratic state based on universal suffrage, and, *second*, the establishment of productive associations of workmen with state subsidies. The proposals were democratic and socialistic, but not revolutionary.

In the *third stage* the revolutionary principle is in full career among the most active and prominent socialists. To this stage belongs the school of Karl Marx, whose ideas as agitator were embodied in the International, the aim of which was to supersede the existing states by a vast combination of the workers of all nations. It may generally be stated that the aim of Social Democracy is to obtain possession of political power, and thus to establish a collectivism from which private property in land and capital is excluded. The Anarchists are another school of revolutionary socialists, who in the International were opposed to the centralising methods of the Marx school, and who, objecting to the principle of authority or compulsion in social organisation, hope to accomplish the renovation of society by the free federation of free associations on the ruins of the existing order of things. Both schools aim at the abolition of the existing state as an organ of the wealthy and privileged class, differing, however, as to the ways and means of accomplishing it.

While all the schools of socialists have based their theories of reconstruction on a criticism of the existing society, this is a special feature of the later schools, especially that of Marx, inasmuch as they have accepted in the fullest sense the scientific doctrine of evolution. Marx appears as agitator and revolutionist in the International, but this is only one side of his activity. No agitation or effort of the revolutionary spirit can produce a change which is inconsistent with the natural tendencies of social evolution. Were socialism not necessitated by the positive forces of the social movement, it might be a seductive theory, but it would be mere Utopianism, and no scientific student of society could support it. So far from being a Utopian dream, socialism, according to Marx, is the inevitable outcome of the movement of modern society. Of this movement Marx is the critic and interpreter. His scientific function is to bring men to a clear consciousness of facts which are establishing themselves, intelligently to see a process which is already going forward in all the countries where the modern industrial methods prevail. The scientific or conscious socialism therefore is merely a reflection or mirroring in the human intelligence of a great world-historic process, which is fulfilling itself, whether we see it or not, whether we will it or not. But the most reluctant must eventually see it and will it, as it must develop its activity till it force itself on the attention of every one, and will urge even the strongest reactionary forward in its irresistible sweep. Science and force can merely assist at the birth of a new social era, which must take place when the time is fulfilled. At the utmost they can only alleviate the pangs of delivery.

Besides those two schools of what may be called militant and aggressive socialism, of which naturally we hear most in the newspapers, and which are by many regarded as the only possible forms of socialism, there are many phases of conservative and Christian socialism that require notice. Christian socialists especially see in our competitive system merely a very modern form of the principle of self-interest degenerating into a selfishness that refuses to be its brother's keeper, and tending to the dissolution of society. While professing to be essential to the continuance and conservation of social order, especially of the Church and family, the present system is in the view of such men subversive of Christian morality and ruinous to all sound and healthy social life. On the other hand, in the much-maligned socialism they find the principle of co-operation and mutual help, which is simply the ethical spirit of Christianity applied to industry and social reform, and would peacefully remedy the evils of competition by promoting associations of workmen with a common capital. Such a form of socialism has been associated both with Catholic and Protestant Christianity, and is and has been a beneficent influence in Germany, Austria, Belgium, France, and England.

Without pretending to a nicety of distinction not justified by broad historic fact, we have offered the above as the leading forms of organised socialism, but we must also refer to the eminent thinkers who, though not belonging to any school or active propaganda, have regarded socialism as the fittest form of economic organisation for the future and the next stage in social evolution. Of these men were J. S. Mill and Rodbertus; and among living representatives the most eminent probably is A. Schäffle, one of the greatest authorities in sociology, especially in the application of evolution to the study of society. Such believers in socialism are to be met with in the most unexpected quarters. We are prepared to find that George Sand was one of them, but it may surprise many that a great critic like Sainte-Beuve expects improvement for the future in the same direction. Moreover, it is a noteworthy fact that most of the recent English political economists have recognised the value of the co-operative system, though they have generally failed to perceive its full import as indicating a new form of industrial organisation fundamentally different from the present. While in many writers, such as Jevons and Cairnes, there is this glimpse of the tendency to a new economic order, in J. S. Mill we have the conscious recognition that English economics must and ought to pass into socialism. Should we regard this as the Utopian side of Mill's teaching, or is it only another proof that he was a man of wider horizon, of keener perception, and of deeper sympathy with struggling humanity than the best of his disciples? The question is worth considering.[1]

[1] For J. S. Mill's deliberate judgment on socialism see his *Autobiography*, pp. 61, 162, 167, &c., and above all his *Political Economy*, chapter on the 'Probable Future of the Labouring Classes.' At his death he left fragments of an unfinished work on socialism, which were published under the title of 'Chapters on Socialism' in the *Fortnightly Review* for 1879. The statement of Schäffle's position given above is based on his *Bau und Leben des socialen Körpers* (1878), a systematic study of society from the evolution point of view, in four vols. In vol. ii. 120 of this work he expresses his belief that 'the future belongs to the purified socialism.' In a small volume (*Hopelessness of the Social-democratic Outlook*, 1885), consisting of three letters addressed to a statesman, and written under the feeling of alarm caused by the progress of the unpurified and revolutionary socialism both in Germany and Austria, Schäffle takes a different attitude. With regard to J. S. Mill, it need scarcely be said that his views on the subject are tentative, as might be expected of a man

In following the development of socialism from its origin in France and England to the present day, nothing impresses us so strongly as the vitality of the movement. Its power of adapting itself to men and nations of the most different condition and temperament, its Protean readiness to assume new forms as circumstances require, have been remarkable. It has disappeared in one decade only to rise up with renewed vigour in the next, and when driven from one country it has forthwith begun to raise its alarming front in another. It is now growing in every civilised country, and in every one it has peculiarities of form and colour. As we have seen, there is a central principle common to all phases of socialism, but in every other respect it is most plastic and adaptive. It is found in connection with the most opposite opinions on other matters, political, social, ethical, and religious. To those who will not take the trouble to distinguish the essence of a movement from its accidental features, it seems the most elusive and contradictory of historical phenomena. Some of its critics seem to regard this as a weakness and a vice. How subject to rational examination theories that are so variable and inconsistent ?

If the great causes of the world had no other purpose than to be the subject merely of disquisition and disputation, if it be the final aim of the massive and living forces of history only to afford material to be analysed and tabulated, we might see some ground

whose mind was continually open to new light and to new possibilities of human progress. Naturally, he does not speak of the future with the confidence of Schäffle. For Sainte-Beuve's views on socialism see his *Vie de Proudhon.*

for such criticism. If socialism were an academic thesis, with no more human application than the latest question of the schools, such an objection would be intelligible enough. Alas! the matter we have to deal with is not so simple as this. The cause of the working man, of which socialism is, rightly or wrongly, a powerful expression, is not a mere theory or formula adapted to the conditions of debate. It represents well or ill the grievances and aspirations after a better life of untold millions of human beings, who toil and suffer under widely different conditions of civilisation. Whether we like it or not, socialism has already a long roll of martyrs and confessors who have been faithful to their convictions under calumny and misrepresentation of the grossest kind, who have died at the barricades, who have pined in exile in tropical swamps and Siberian mines. Socialism is a contemporary manifestation of social grievance which has through long generations been borne by the sweating millions of labour that have endured patiently and died in silent misery, leaving no record of their awful burden of sorrow. It is the cause of wretched multitudes of men and women and children that has at last found utterance and organisation, the protest of workers that still suffer from excessive hours of monotonous drudgery in mine and factory in many lands, who live in economic insecurity and degradation, surrounded by the superabundant wealth which their toil has created. Surely the proceedings of such a movement cannot reasonably be expected to conform to any academic rule.

Moreover, in estimating the success or failure of a movement we should have regard to the magnitude of the task it undertakes. Socialism aims at achieving a vast transformation in the theory and practice of human affairs. The first efforts towards such a great result must of necessity be doubtful and tentative. In this respect the career of Robert Owen may be taken as a sample of the whole movement. If Owen had followed the beaten routine he would have been celebrated as the first cotton-spinner and the most notable philanthropist of his day, and would probably have died a millionaire and a member of the House of Lords. But he dared to be original in his schemes of philanthropic reform, and failed. Are not the failures of some men greater than the most eminent success of the ordinary kind ?

When we consider the magnitude of the problem which it attempts to solve, when we contemplate the seething and fermenting forces of which it is the expression, we need not wonder that socialism takes so many forms. Its plasticity and adaptiveness are to be reckoned among the first elements of its strength. It cannot be fixed in a dogma. It cannot be identified with the theories of any single thinker. It grows out of real and living forces, ethical, political, and industrial, which compel fresh inquiry and experiment in all directions. Such a movement, with its robust strength, its exhaustless vitality and rapid development, cannot be reduced to a formula.

There can be no doubt that socialism is only a pronounced and notable phase of a larger movement. On the ethical side it is the outcome, exaggerated and unreasonable it may be, of a strong aspiration for a higher life among the workers. In times that are still recent, the moral consciousness of man has received a new elevation and expansion. We have awakened to the fact that the majority of the human family, including most women and the working classes, have been virtually shut out from all participation in the world's inheritance of knowledge and culture. Woman has seldom been the free and worthy companion of man. From time immemorial the labouring classes have been sunk in drudgery and ignorance, bearing the burden of society without sharing in its happiness. Neither woman nor worker has had any substantial part in a free, healthy, and well-developed life, in which mind and body receive just and adequate attention. In the French Revolution a great change was proclaimed, in which the watchwords of liberty, equality, and fraternity announced a complete reversal of the old injustice. Cynics and disbelievers in human progress will still laugh at the wild unreality of these ideals. Yet we all believe in freedom, and fraternity is one of the precepts of Christianity. As to equality, Christianity goes farther than the Revolution; it requires that we be servants one of another, it insists on the law of mutual service.

Such ideals assuredly will never die out in the world. The best and noblest hearts will always return to them with fresh yearning for their realisation, and there is, let us hope, a very substantial sense in which the experience of men will find them true and sound. What many are beginning to see is that such ideals require for their realisation a solid economic basis. Without a corresponding economic change the best ethical and social aspirations cannot be realised. What value have such brilliant watchwords to a starving proletariat? What is the meaning of human brotherhood, when the existing arrangements of property are such as to make the word a mockery? Without a great economic change, our much-vaunted freedom is also wanting in solidity and efficacy; is only another dearly cherished delusion. Is socialism the economic complement of the French Revolution?

However it be as regards socialism, there can be no doubt that, apart from the cynics, the sceptics, incorrigible doctrinaires, and mere men of the world, there is a growing spirit of righteous discontent with our social and economic arrangements. Our present condition, strongly fortified though it be by prescription and the conservatism of vested rights, is hopelessly at variance with the moral sense of the *élite* of men, who have always been the pioneers of progress. The same spirit more and more pervades the mass of serious and thinking men. That spirit has descended to the people, and is there accentuated by deep and acute feeling of long unmerited suffering. It may be that the condition of the workmen has greatly improved in most countries during the last fifty years, but it is very doubtful whether their economic improvement has kept pace with their advancing intelligence and the growing sense of their rights and claims. There can be no doubt that their condition is still, in many countries, extremely bad, and that we may discern among them a growing enlightenment, greater power of organisation, a higher feeling of what is right and due, a stronger aspiration after higher things, and that all this intellectual and ethical development impresses on them every day a sharper consciousness of the contrast between their actual state and the better life to which they ought to attain. This opposition of the progressive ethical and social spirit to the established economic order, with its faulty arrangements handed down from the past, is one of the most significant facts of our time.

For we must recognise the fact that the economic arrangements now prevailing in most civilised countries were made at a time when the mass of the people had no share in education, legislation, or government, and when they were not permitted to organise in defence of their rights. Is it not natural, then, that they should find these arrangements most unsatisfactory, and that the spirit of social innovation is abroad?

In connection with this, few men realise the vast influence likely to be exercised on our economic and social condition by the growth of democracy. During the last generation the mass of the people in most civilised countries have for the first time been admitted to a share in political power. As is just and fitting, the right of universal suffrage has been associated with universal education. At the same time, the cheap newspaper and the diffusion of cheap literature have brought political and all other forms of knowledge within the reach of the lowest of the people. The extension of the railway system, of cheap postage, and of cheap telegraphic communication has given them facilities for common action and organisation which they never possessed before. By many it may not be considered a very desirable thing that the duty of bearing arms has also become universal on the continent of Europe; but in the wide and incessant rise of democracy it is a most important fact that the old professional soldiery has given place to a national army which must continue to be greatly in sympathy with the mass of the people. The armed support of the rulers of Europe now consists of educated citizens, who are not long enough with the flag to be dissociated from popular feeling.

These are elementary facts known to every one. But we do not sufficiently realise the far-reaching influence that they are calculated to exercise on our whole social development. Many are disappointed because the democracy, while holding the form of power, is content to leave the substance in the hands of the old parties. Such men are strangely ignorant of the facts and conditions of the question. Some of us seem to have already forgotten the low estate out of which we emerged not many years ago; how short a time it is since education became general and anything like a real stimulus was given to the intelligence of the people. There always is a class of impatient workers, who would like to reap the harvest before they have sown the seed. It is the exceeding lateness of the sowing that we must all lament. It will ever excite wonder and amazement that a country which has so long claimed to be in the van of progress did not establish a national system of education till 1870. Nearly four centuries have passed away since England through the Protestant Reformation declared that light was better than darkness, and so slow have we been in seeing that light was better for the mass of the people!

It would be well that our energetic friends should have a little patience with the people. The evil habits bred by immemorial ignorance and servitude cannot be thrown off in a day. Long years, generations perhaps, must pass before the new influences can have exhausted or even fairly developed themselves. The results likely to be evolved through the rise of an educated and organised democracy establishing itself under potent conditions all over the civilised world cannot be measured and tabulated in the first generation. We see a multitude of new forces, each of which is powerful, the combined influence of which no man can calculate. Of the era into which through such conditions we are marching, we can but say that it will be different from anything the world has yet produced, and that the efforts to confine the new order within the conventional limits and to direct it along the old lines will be in vain. The democratic movement is just beginning, and it is rather early to pass sentence upon it; but of this at least we may be sure, that the people who think that the democracy consists of vote by ballot, and that everything else will proceed in the old style, will be grievously disappointed.

The democratic movement is a vast complexity of living forces which cannot be reduced to a formula. It is a solid and massive movement made up of many contributing influences. Social progress and the march of history do not move on isolated lines. Soul and body, the physical and intellectual growth of man, the inner and outer life of society, the moral and material development of history and of civilisation must be contemplated as a whole. There can be no real political advance without a corresponding moral improvement, and both should rest on a sound economic basis. Not each nation only, but the whole human society, under the conditions which now prevail, is a vast organism, a body of many members with a mutual life. It is quite misleading to consider man and his circumstances in isolation; to regard him apart from the past out of which he has grown, or from the present of which he is a unit.

We should, therefore, strongly recommend the confident and dogmatic people who undertake to measure the new democracy, to lay their formulas aside and keep their eyes open. Even for them the coming time may bring a few lessons. The problem is a complex one, which should be approached from many points of view and treated by a catholic variety of methods. Only let them proceed on a sympathetic consideration of the real conditions of the case. Everything that tends to raise man in soul, body, or estate should be encouraged.

The formulas both of criticism and of reform drawn from the experience of the past and dogmatically applied to the modern democracy are, therefore, likely to fail us. But there is a special reason why men should keep their minds open for the reception of new light. It is the supreme interest of all that the course of change should not degenerate into violence, and nothing is more likely to bring about such a fatal issue than obstinate resistance to reform when confronted with the headstrong and unreasoning spirit of innovation. Perhaps there is hardly a violent movement in the past that has done any real good. Violence has generally intervened only to mar the work of wise and moderate change. At these crises men have so often opposed each other, who were fitted to co-operate for the common advantage.

Besides the fearful havoc they caused at the time, revolutions have usually led to strong reaction, to moral lassitude and the dull prison-house of apathy and despair. Probably there is not a violent revolution in history that one can contemplate with a solid and genuine approval.

Of those who drew the sword at the Reformation, how many, whether victors or vanquished, derived any conspicuous benefit from the struggle ? In Germany it ended in the horrors of the Thirty Years' War. In France there were civil wars for a generation, and when Protestantism was at last dragooned and expelled, did Catholic France gain by driving out so many of her best subjects ? The Scots were always obstinately in the right, and refused to be reasonable even with Cromwell, and fell into narrowness, uncharitableness, and insensibility to the beautiful in worship and in common life. By means it may be of inglorious compromises, England had the greatest success in wedding the best of the new to the best of the old. There is a convenience in believing that one's opponents are of the devil, but it is a convenience frequently purchased at the expense of truth and charity. For the comprehension of history, charity is almost as essential as the scientific spirit. He is merely a partisan whose sympathies are all on one side. We can entirely love and admire only the peaceful victories of reason and of the progressive wisdom and goodness, and of these no revolutionary party can claim a monopoly. The parties are generally champions of half-truths and incomplete virtues. There may be critical and decisive moments in the history of the world when good men must choose a side ; but they are not the worst who have hesitated most before taking the final step.

Let us hope, then, that the modern democracy, while it fulfils its mission with fitting energy, will rule with moderation and dignity. A quiet and temperate power is the best, and in the long run the most effective.

In this country we are accustomed to peaceful and constitutional methods of action, and though the progress is lamentably slow, our experience as compared with that of other lands entirely justifies the course we have pursued. While we have been comparatively free from the violence so frequently attendant on social change, we are in most respects ahead of our neighbours. But it may be that we have special cause of anxiety for the future. The industrial revolution brought about by mechanical invention was for a long time worked out chiefly in England, and has most powerfully affected the national life. One of its most prominent effects has been to call into existence a vast number of workers almost entirely dependent on wage-labour, which is often precarious and irregular. Our large towns are swarming with workers who have no capital and live from hand to mouth. Even in ordinary times a sudden change of industry may throw thousands of them out of the employment which is their only resource ; in times of depression the outlook grows extremely dark. In the rural districts we find the same general divorce of the workmen from the means of production. No country of the world has in proportion to its size such a host of workers divorced from land and capital, without control of the conditions under which they labour, and living in economic insecurity. This is probably the most conspicuous result of the industrial revolution and of that marvellous supremacy in the markets of the world, of which we were once so proud, which at one time promised so much. It is not a particularly glorious consummation. Nor is there any marked sign of improvement. Our rural workers still keep flocking to the large towns. In spite of a very considerable emigration and a declining birth-rate, our population increases by about half a million every year. Who can believe that the expansion of our industries will keep pace with such an expansion of population ? In the poor of London and our large towns a question is advancing upon us in comparison with which that of Ireland is a bright and hopeful one.

It is true we had the statistics of Mr. Giffen, showing how the working classes had improved during the fifty years before he wrote. Of the general improvement, especially among the skilled and organised workmen, there can be no doubt ; but there are many circumstances relating to our industrial development which very materially lessen the hope and comfort derivable from such figures. In the first place, the period adopted for comparison with the present was 1830–1840, when, as Mr. Giffen himself explains, the condition of labour was extremely low. Indeed, it seems to be universally admitted that the period from 1780 to 1840 was the worst in the history of the English labourer since the feudal system began to decline in the middle of the fourteenth century. How then can we draw any solid comfort from such comparisons ?

We should also remember that the period since 1850 has been a time of industrial expansion connected with opportunities for energetic workmen that the world has never before seen, and such, in many essential respects, as we can never again see. During that time the railway and telegraph systems have been extended over the whole civilised world. Sailing vessels have been superseded by steamships. The machine industry which we devised has been carried to other lands. Water and gas, and other appliances of modern life, have been introduced into the towns. In all these great industrial undertakings Englishmen led the way and gained the firstfruits to be derived from new enterprises. A colonial expansion on a corresponding scale has taken place at the same time. Steamships have conveyed across the seas hundreds of thousands of energetic colonists who under other circumstances might have been discontented at home. The goldfields of California and Victoria, the gigantic valley of the Mississippi, and the wide expanse of the North-west, as well as the vast pastoral and agricultural regions of Australia, have been exploited by the Anglo-Saxon. These are only the most marked features of a marvellous expansion which has embraced the whole world; and a combination of fortunate conditions has given Englishmen and the cognate Americans the first place in the great movement. No wonder Chartism died out! It would have been fearful if the English workman had not won a small share in this spoliation of the world.

But according to all human probability, this expansion is a most exceptional phenomenon. The world will not require a new railway system every generation; and each country is learning to keep its own lines in working order. We must not expect that we shall again be the teachers of mankind in an industrial revolution. At any rate, there are no more Mississippi valleys in this planet lying unoccupied and unexploited since the birth of time; and there is only one Australia. There is, indeed, much unoccupied room in this planet; but no such extraordinary opportunities as we had in 1850. Our success in the past is no proof that our economic and industrial methods are to be accepted as good for the time coming.

Moreover, the improved condition of the workmen has been due largely to better organisation among themselves, and to the beneficent intervention of society. The period from 1780 to 1840 was also a period of expansion, but it was a time when the workers were ignorant, lacking in organisation, and without protection from society. It was a time of wretchedness for labour but of rapid accumulation of wealth by the capitalists and landlords. The period since 1850 has seen the development of trade unions and co-operation, the diffusion of education, and the operation of the Factory Acts. All of these are forms of social organisation and control. It would seem that it is in this direction and not in the assertion of individualism that improvement may be attained.

The period since 1850 has, therefore, been a record of progress, gained largely through exceptional opportunities of expansion. And we must face the fact that we have an enormous population dependent on the precarious demands of a labour market which cannot possibly expand in the future as it has done in the past. Countries which were once our customers have become our rivals. Our industrial supremacy, once absolutely unquestioned, is now disputed in various markets by Germany, Belgium, France, and America.

For the difficulties of the new time there is no panacea. It is impossible there can be any panacea except the very old and comprehensive one that every man and institution in the country endeavour to do their duty. Fortunately there is amongst us a growing spirit of reasonable and energetic reform. We are agreed that social troubles cannot be met by obstinate resistance, nor can they be removed by stormy and fanatical change. We can expect to succeed only by the freest discussion of social and economic questions, and by the wise and energetic adaptation of our institutions to the necessities of the time. Nothing is so trying to the unreason of innovation as to be subjected to calm and dispassionate inquiry. Nothing is so disconcerting to a hoary abuse as to turn the full light of day upon it. The fanaticism of revolution and the fanaticism of reaction will both disappear under the wholesome and searching influences of truth and fact.

In view of all the foregoing considerations it is imperative that we examine the claims of socialism in a spirit of fairness. But we shall be better able to do so if we learn to understand the origin and nature of the present system.

CHAPTER II

RISE OF THE PRESENT SYSTEM

As we have seen, England led the way in the industrial revolution by which the present social and economic system was introduced. In England, therefore, we must study its rise and progress. It arose by a gradual process of development out of the mediæval order of society. The mediæval order was characterised by two great institutions, feudalism and the Catholic Church.

Under the feudal system the tillers of the soil rendered to their superiors customary dues both in kind and in labour. At the beginning of the fourteenth century money rents began to take the place of the old customary dues. Thus early did a cash nexus supersede the old relation of dependence of the tenant on his lord. In the Wars of the Roses during the latter half of the fifteenth century the feudal nobility was for the most part destroyed; and the strongly centralised rule of Edward IV. and the Tudors was established. Round the Tudor dynasty a court nobility grew up instead of the old feudal nobility. Whereas in feudal times the power of the noble depended on the number and efficiency of the fighting men he could bring into the field, the influence of the court noble depended chiefly on the length of his rent-roll. He was forbidden by law to maintain bands of retainers as formerly, and indeed he had now no particular interest in keeping them. They were therefore broken up, and the old fighting men became a useless and dangerous class of idlers.

A great rise in the price of wool, which marked the early part of the sixteenth century, increased the tendency to adopt the merely commercial use of land. The landlords found it more profitable to convert the small holdings of the peasantry into sheep-runs. Inclosures led to evictions, by which vast numbers were driven from the soil and forced into a life of vagabondage. When the monasteries were broken up and the Church lands were seized by Henry VIII. and his courtiers, things became very much worse. The fall of feudalism and of the Catholic Church thus meant the dissolution of an ancient society, the effects of which it is hardly possible for us to realise.

Here we are concerned chiefly with its influence on the social and economic life of the mass of the people. Commercial ideas as to the use of land had become supreme. Reasons of State and of good government of the most convincing and urgent nature there might be that the rural population should not be turned adrift into poverty and vagrancy. But the political and legal power rested entirely with the King, and with his courtiers and privy councillors, who were or aspired to be landholders. The private interest of the landowning class determined the general course of social economic development. Reasons of State and the good of the people were alike put aside. Legislation to check inclosures, which was repeatedly passed during a long period of years, had little permanent effect, because those who were able to enforce the laws were interested in setting them aside. The few risings that took place were put down by the nobles with the aid of foreign mercenaries.

During this vast process of change, which continued for about a century, the people were for the most part not only unorganised, but voiceless. Yet we have some clear glimpses of their condition. Most vivid are the references to it in the introduction to More's 'Utopia.' Those mild animals, the sheep, we are told, had begun to devour men and unpeople not only villages but towns. To make room for them thousands of acres were inclosed by some insatiable wretch; and owners as well as tenants were turned out by force or fraud or wearied by repeated wrongs into parting with their property. Men and women, old and young, were driven from their homes, not knowing where to go. They were obliged to sell their household stuff almost for nothing, and the money being soon spent, they had no resource but to steal and be hanged for it, or to go about and beg. In this way began that process of eviction which continued in Ireland and the Highlands of Scotland till the nineteenth century. The cultivators of the soil under a feudal or a clan system were expelled under pressure of a new system, in which money considerations were supreme.

The landholding class, which had thus forced the poor people into vagabondage, proceeded by a course of savage legislation to cure the evil, now become national, which they had themselves created. Vagabonds were whipped; they were put in the stocks, or in the pillory, where they had their ears cut off; and they were hanged in rows twenty at a time. By an Act passed in the reign of Edward VI., which, however, was repealed in two years, they could even be reduced to slavery.

Such industry apart from agriculture as existed in mediæval times was organised in guilds, which were combinations of merchants and craftsmen for the defence and promotion of their common interests at a time when law and order were not securely established. The separation of these industrialists into the two classes of employer and employed had not yet declared itself. Apprentice, journeyman, and master were generally speaking merely three stages in the career of the worker. But the property of these guilds was also confiscated by Henry VIII. and the nobles who ruled in the name of his son Edward. In the course of time the guild system broke down. The action of the new central power, which sought to regulate industry in all its departments, was not favourable to self-governing local industry. Thus the mediæval organisation of industry was dissolved. Many influences contributed to introduce a division of interests among the industrialists, with the general result that a class of employers distinct from the employed was finally constituted. The workmen were everywhere treated as an inferior class, being without education or political rights, and crushed under a load of oppressive legislative enactments and adverse social and economic conditions.

We can now see how rural life and town life alike felt the far-reaching effects of this revolution. Throughout the country the castles of the feudal nobles and the abbeys and other religious houses had been centres of busy life. Nobles like the famous Earl of Warwick the Kingmaker had great numbers of retainers, tenants, and all manner of dependants. The religious houses were centres of arts and crafts, of hospitality and of almsgiving, as well as of religion. In the course of the revolution feudal retainers and tenants, the monks and their tenants and dependants, lost their means of living, and were driven loose from their old moorings. Their homes and their customary habits of life were alike cruelly broken up. Even if they had been able and willing to work, the labour market of those days was totally inadequate to absorb the numbers thus cast adrift. Wages, compared with the price of food, were miserably low. Towns decayed, and rural life sank to a low level both in interest and activity. It was not till the reign of Elizabeth that things began to settle down under the new conditions. By the middle of the seventeenth century, according to the estimate of Thorold Rogers, at least half the population of England was dependent on weekly wages.

The main effect of these changes was that the mediæval organisation of society, resting on the manor and the guild under the feudal and Catholic systems, was destroyed to make way for the system which now prevails.

After a long period of preparation and gradual development the forces of change set in with special rapidity and intensity about the middle of the eighteenth century. An industrial revolution associated with mechanical invention, with the application of steam as the motive power, and with the rise of the factory system, then definitely began, and is still proceeding in almost every country of the world.

A variety of causes combined to make England the first great scene of its activity. She was supreme on the sea, and had driven her rivals, both French and Dutch, out of North America and East India. She had a considerable share of the West Indies, at that time a colonial possession of much greater importance than now. Liverpool and Bristol took a leading part in the lucrative and nefarious slave trade. Thus England had established a vast colonial empire, secured by her domination of the seas; and she had won for herself an ever-growing commerce and markets in every part of the world, which were continually widening. The wars in which we were incessantly engaged from the revolution of 1689 to Waterloo were fought out abroad, and did not materially interfere with the development of our industries—in fact most effectually promoted them by extending and securing our markets. While the nations of the Continent were devastated and exhausted by long wars waged on their own territory, the soil of England was free from foreign armies. Within her own borders there was peace, under the shadow of which she had time to accumulate an immense capital, and to train a numerous class of workmen in the new methods of industry. We had nearly a hundred years of this industrial progress before Germany, so long disunited and overrun by foreign armies, could enter upon the race.

At home a variety of other causes tended not less powerfully towards the development of the new system of industry. That we had coal and iron and other minerals necessary for it in great abundance and in close proximity to each other is a familiar fact. We have a climate suited to a laborious industry, and a geographical position favourable to a wide commerce and to the development of colonial enterprise. Religious and political discontent even more than the spirit of enterprise urged large numbers of the people during the seventeenth century to seek the freer and larger field of opportunity beyond the ocean. We have already referred to the process by which the working people of England were divorced from the soil on the downfall of feudalism and of the Catholic Church. Of this process historical science will in the future have much to say. It had one clear result of the greatest importance, to deprive a large mass of the population of a fixed interest in the soil, to drive them into the towns, and thus to prepare for the coming time a numerous class which as workers or capitalists would carry on the new industrialism.

It was a condition of things in which the natural advantages and resources of the country conspired with the tendencies of our social development to give England the first place in the industrial revolution. Our success has been set down to different causes more or less flattering to the national pride. It is supposed to have been greatly due to the peculiar sagacity, energy, and love of freedom of the English race; and it is true that we possess a considerable share of these desirable qualities, but without any conspicuous superiority to the French and Germans. In view of our immense advantages both natural and historical, in view of our enormous mineral wealth and our insular position, which has protected us from the worst consequences of Continental warfare, such explanations have no serious importance.

For generations our markets had been extending, and the love of gain had been whetted by the tribute both of the East and West. The old methods of industry were unable to keep pace with the demands of a market so rapidly growing and with the insatiable spirit of acquisition. New and more powerful productive forces were required. A potent stimulus was thus given to the inventive spirit, which, after long experiment and unsuccessful effort, at last supplied the want with mechanical appliances connected with the names of Hargreaves, Arkwright, and Crompton. Above all, a new motive power for the new machinery was found by James Watt, the greatest innovator and revolutionist the world has ever seen. The work formerly done by the human hand, by horse-power, or by the uncertain forces of wind and water, was now performed by steam, a strong and regular agency, which can be created as required, and works both in summer and winter, in perfect obedience to the guiding hand of man. In a few decades the methods and conditions of industry and of social life were entirely changed. The spinning-wheel gave way to the spinning-jenny. The hand-loom was driven out by the power-loom. The stage-coach was superseded by the railway train, the sailing-vessel by the steamship. The application of steam to printing gave us cheap literature and the penny newspaper. Such are a few of the features of the industrial revolution. Society was established on a new technical basis.

Even the proximate results of the industrial revolution in the history of England were incalculable. It gave employment to vast numbers of new workmen. Many of the capitalists who were successful in the struggle for wealth made vast fortunes out of trade. The growing demand for agricultural produce on the part of the increasing industrial population, intensified as it was by our exclusion from foreign markets by wars and corn-laws, led to an enormous rise of rents and to a rapid expansion of cultivation. The landowners and the industrial magnates, and adventurers enriched with the spoils of the East and West, carried their well-filled coffers to the House of Lords. The new industry furnished Britain with the resources for carrying on the gigantic struggle with Napoleon. And it cheapened the products of industry, creating and multiplying to a marvellous degree all the means and appliances of happiness and culture.

One most important result of the industrial revolution was to concentrate industry in the hands of a limited number of capitalists. Industry was now organised on a large scale in factories. The capitalist who could provide himself with steam-power and the best machinery, who could most skilfully and energetically take advantage of the division and organisation of labour, had a crushing superiority over the isolated producer working on the old methods. In this way a large system of industry was established, by which the small producer was completely overborne in the competitive struggle. The spinning was transferred from the cottage to the factory. The hand-loom weaver was slowly starved out before the power-loom. The small farmer, too, was out of date. In every department the most economical and effective methods of industry prevailed.

From the beginning of the industrial revolution it was apparent, however, that the new system was oppressive alike to the workers whom it employed, and to the small producer whom it superseded. Along with steam-power and the new machinery cheap labour was the great desideratum of the capitalist in the competition which now ensued. Cheap labour was accordingly mercilessly utilised in factory organisation. Hence the systematic employment of women and children to tend the new machinery in the factories. In order to provide a sufficiency of such cheap labour the owners of factories entered into contracts with the Poor-Law Guardians of London and other places, by which batches of children were forwarded to the industrial centres ; in some cases it was agreed that an idiot should be taken for every nineteen of sound mind. These poor creatures were worked for twelve or even fifteen hours a day, and were often cruelly beaten by the overseers. Many of the children were taken into the mills at the age of five or six, sometimes earlier. Without parental oversight, without education, demoralised by weary drudgery under insanitary conditions, badly fed and badly housed, we need not wonder that they grew up to be morally and physically degenerate, and that their offspring was no better. Mothers employed for very long hours in factories, and without the most elementary knowledge of their domestic duties, were not likely to bring up good and healthy children. Apart from more terrible evils, the physique of England must have permanently suffered from the abuses of our industrialism. Altogether, even the soberest record of our factory system is too revolting for belief and even description. By such methods were the industrial glories of England established and enormous fortunes made—out of the groans, and tears, and degradation of innocent children and helpless women.[1]

But the fearful contrast of accumulating wealth and unspeakable misery was not confined to the factory system. Mining was probably worse, and agriculture was no better. During the whole course of the great war with Napoleon rents increased enormously, the process of money-making going forward on a basis of misery. During the war the rental of Scotland rose from 2,000,000*l*. a year to about 5,278,000*l*. The rent of farms in Essex increased at the same time from 10*s*. to 45*s*. and even 50*s*. per acre; in Berkshire and Wiltshire from 14*s*. to 70*s*. per acre. In these years the price of wheat rose again and again to famine prices: in 1795 it was 126*s*., in 1801 it rose to 139*s*. and even 180*s*. per quarter; in 1812 it again stood at 126*s*. per quarter. It might reasonably be expected that wages must have risen in something like a tolerable proportion to the rise in the price of the staple food, but the advance was confined to skilled artisans, and in their case it was only partial.[2]

[1] The record of the shame, and it should also be said of the penitence, of England is told in the annals of the factory and other legislation, especially in the various parliamentary reports. The early results of the industrial revolution are described in Porter's *Progress of the Nation*. The influence of the same revolution has been worked out with great power and elaboration by Karl Marx in his *Capital*. For an impartial and moderate account of its results, see Spencer Walpole's *History of England since 1815*.

[2] 'In some few cases there had been an advance of wages, but this occurred only to skilled artisans, and even with them the rise was wholly incommensurate with the increased cost of all the necessaries of life. The mere labourer—he who has nothing to bring to market but his limbs and sinews—did not participate in this partial compensation for high prices, but was in most cases an eager

After the war, though rents fell very considerably, they were still greatly in advance of what they had previously been, while the misery of the people steadily continued both in town and country, in some years swelling to an unbearable degree of intensity. The wretchedness of the workers culminated in the fearful years about 1840. We need not here repeat the harrowing tale of the wretchedness which then prevailed among our industrial population. Miserable dwellings, towns in which the laws of sanitation were set at defiance, food of the worst quality, and frequently not to be had at all, incredible ignorance, moods of despair alternating with the spirit of angry revolt and riot—such were the too prevalent features in the condition of the working classes. Chartism was simply the expression of the dire agony of English labour in its long death-wrestle with disease, starvation, and ignorance.

Of all the phenomena connected with the industrial revolution nothing is so striking and characteristic as the fate of the hand-loom weavers. Though invented by Cartwright in 1787, the power-loom was not put to practical use till 1801, and it was some years later before it began to be a dangerous rival of the hand-loom. Thus for several decades after the invention of the new methods of spinning, and the application of steam to machinery, the hand-loom continued to

competitor for employment at the same, or nearly the same, wages as had been given before the war. There was a superabundant supply of labourers constantly competing for employment at the large government establishments, where the weekly wages did not exceed 15*s.*, while the price of the quartern loaf was 1*s.* 10*d.*, and the other necessary outgoings of a labourer's family were nearly as high in proportion.'—Porter, vol. ii. 283.

be the sole or chief means of weaving. Consequently a large number of weavers were required to supply the greatly increased demand that had sprung up under the new conditions. It is estimated that in 1833 there were 250,000 hand-loom weavers in Great Britain, and 800,000 persons dependent on this industry. By that time, however, the hand-loom was doomed. It is one of the acknowledged evils of the new system that the workman is part of a great industrial mechanism, that in the division of labour he learns his own particular function and nothing else; but that if a change occurs rendering his particular work unnecessary he is helpless and exposed to ruin. This was the fate of the poor hand-loom weavers, whose agony, prolonged by poor-relief, on 2½*d.* a day, is one of the saddest chapters of the industrial revolution.

But the evil results of the new industrial competition were not confined to our own country. The demand for raw cotton by our rapidly growing mills greatly stimulated its production in America. American slavery assumed a harder and crueller aspect. The inordinate love of gain that impelled men to overtask the poor children in English factories could not be resisted by the slave-owners in the Southern States, and the system of working out their hands in seven years was introduced. The poor negro, toiling amidst the swamps of Alabama or Louisiana under the lash of a Legree, felt the influence of the new industrial system. In spite of protection our industrial supremacy exercised a severe pressure on the workers of the Continent; and in India, where protection did not exist, it whitened the plains with the bones of the cottage-weavers.

We have heard much of the blessings conferred on mankind through the industrial progress of the last hundred years, how it has extended the control of man over the resources of nature, and multiplied all the necessaries of life; how it has given us railways, the electric telegraph, cheap books, cheap newspapers, gas, an efficient water supply, and a thousand other appliances of a higher and better civilisation. All this it has done to a marvellous degree. But let us not forget that especially in its earlier stages the industrial revolution acted without social or ethical control, and, being made the instrument of private gain, resulted in the excessive enrichment of the few, and in the impoverishment and degradation of the many. Unless the material and technical appliances of civilisation are subordinate to moral ends and to the promotion of true social well-being, we have no guarantee that their influence will be beneficial. Like the natural forces, steam and electricity, by which it is moved, the mechanism of the industrial revolution must be directed by intelligence acting on principles of justice and humanity, in order that it be a true instrument of progress. If the triumphs of mechanical invention are only to be weapons for more effectually subjecting and exploiting the masses of mankind, better that James Watt had never succeeded with the steam-engine. Under the new system, as under the old, the ethical factor is the dominant one. The supreme question must be, how to make the new industrial forces subservient to the good of men.

The rulers and leaders of England had other work to do than to control the industrial revolution for the good of the people. While Watt was perfecting the steam-engine they were preparing to coerce the American colonies. Later on, when the new industrial system was developing into its colossal manhood, they were fighting the French and maintaining the corn-laws. On the whole, the new system was left to the free energy of the industrialists, and it degenerated into a rapacious scramble for wealth, from which a favoured few emerged successful.

Before long it became evident that a new division of classes had become permanently established in England. Having no fixed interest in the soil of his native country, finding that, with his small and rude means of production, he could no longer compete against machinery, the workman was fain to enrol himself in the service of the capitalist. Naturally he found a difficulty in adapting himself to the tedious and demoralising drudgery of a mill. But necessity, in the form of hunger, quelled his courage. A population of workers suited to the new conditions rapidly grew up, a population that too generally was drunken, thriftless, and thoughtless, of poor physique and poor morale. It was, indeed, one of the worst evils of the industrial revolution that it so powerfully stimulated the growth of such a class. In large and populous districts not a public school existed. Thus a gigantic industrialism was established, marked on the one hand by successful capitalists, who grew enormously wealthy, and on the other by a vast host of working men divorced from land and capital, exposed to all the vicissitudes of an ever-changing trade, over which they had no more control than over a hurricane or an earthquake, often without a fixed home, their family life broken up by the despotic requirements of the factory.

The most striking results of the industrial revolution have therefore been : *first*, the concentration of industry in the hands of successful capitalists ; *second*, the creation of the modern proletariat. The last word is not here used as a term of reproach. It is a sufficiently accurate name for a class of workers who have practically nothing to depend on but wage-labour that is often precarious and inadequate. Be it also remembered that the period of worst degradation and impoverishment for English labour coincided with the most marvellous development of riches that the world had seen up to that date, that is to say, with the period from 1780 to 1850, from the time steam came into effective play till the middle of the last century. Against this sad destiny the individual worker could do little to protect himself. He was at the mercy of forces over which he had only the most limited control. He had before him the alternative either to rise to be a capitalist, using other men's labour, or to be a labourer used by a capitalist. The former alternative could fall only to a very few. The mass sank into a condition of economic dependency. For we must emphasise the fact that the isolated worker of the olden time, with his small means of production, had to disappear in proportion as the revolution extended. It was a struggle between the isolated workman using his own small capital, and the large industry. The victory was to the latter, to the large system of production with machinery moved by steam, with large numbers of workmen organised and directed by capitalists competing for their own profit. The independent workman, utilising his own capital, had on the whole to disappear.

The revolution, which began in England, as we have seen, still goes forward, and is extending over the whole world. In almost every European country it is establishing itself. Distant countries, which were once merely the markets and producers of raw material for England, are beginning to adopt the methods of the new industry. This India is doing; and even China, which so long excluded European influences, is now ready to introduce railways, telegraphs, and the other appliances of the West. Her long hesitation was probably due not only to the fear of political interference on the part of foreign powers, but of having her own social system disturbed by the new industry. If the hand-loom weavers of England suffered so much from the changes made by mechanical invention, what will be the fate of the craftsmen of China with their backward methods of production?

In this world-revolution steam has become a comparatively old agent, and has been reinforced by electricity, marking a further advance in the dominion of man over nature. James Watt, patiently devising means for applying steam to the service of man, and Benjamin Franklin compelling the lightning from the clouds, are the worthy representatives of the new era.

In no country of the world has the new industrialism made such gigantic strides as in America. A paper drawn up by a committee of the American Social Science Association, and read at its meeting in Cincinnati in 1878, depicts with great vividness the change made by labour-saving machinery in the United States. In agriculture, the old wooden plough is of course replaced by the steam-plough; sowing, formerly done by hand, is now done by machinery. On the vast prairie lands of the Mississippi and in California the grain is cut by reapers with cutters which are ten, twelve, eighteen, and even twenty-four feet long.

To such a degree of perfection is the mechanism for harvesting brought that 'in California machines are made and used, which at one and the same time, in moving over the field, cut the grain, thresh, winnow, and sack it, and the filled sacks are left in rows where, but a few moments before, stood the golden grain untouched, inviting to its harvest.' So with all the other operations of American husbandry: 'machinery digs potatoes, milks the cows, makes the butter and cheese.'

In the carriage of agricultural products to the great centres of population a similar revolution has been effected. 'Even our cattle and hogs are no longer required to walk to the shambles; the iron horse takes them to the butcher, labour-saving processes slaughter them, dress them, prepare their flesh for the market, for the table, and stop only at mastication, deglutition, and digestion.

'To-day, one man with the aid of machinery will produce as much food as could be produced by the naked muscle and tools of a score of our fathers. There is now no known limit to the power of its production. In consumption there is no corresponding increase. Our fathers required, obtained, and used as many ounces of food per day as we do. It might have been different in kind and quality—nothing more.

'Not long ago the farm found constant employment for all the sons of the farm and many of the children of the city. Now, the farm furnishes employment for but a very small number of its sons, and that for a very few weeks or months at most in the year, and for the rest work must be had in the cities and towns, or not at all.

'Here we find the true reason for the stagnation in the population of the older agricultural sections, and abnormal growth and crowding of the cities.'

Formerly the farmers raised their own wool and flax, which were spun and woven into cloth by the members of their household. Now all is changed. Carding, spinning, weaving, knitting, and sewing are done by machinery.

In all the operations of building and carpentry we see a like change. 'Machinery does nine-tenths of the labour, and muscle the little remainder.'

Boots and shoes are now made by machinery. The introduction of machinery into the watch trade is superseding the hand watchmakers of England and Switzerland. The operations of mining and engineering are carried on with the aid of powerful machinery.

The paper of the American Social Science Association then goes on to explain the general results of the industrial revolution in that country in the following manner:

'Now, let us see what have been the general effects which have resulted from the use of labour-saving machinery. I will briefly sum them up in a few distinct conclusions.

'1. It has broken up and destroyed our whole system of agriculture as practised by our fathers, which required the whole time and attention of all the sons of the farm and many from the towns, in the never-ending duties of food production, and has driven them to the towns and cities to hunt for employment, or remain in great part idle.

'2. It has broken up and destroyed our whole system of household and family manufactures, as done by our mothers, when all took part in the labour and shared in the product, to the comfort of all; and has compelled the daughters of our country and towns to factory operations for ten or twelve hours a day in the manufacture of cloth they may not wear, though next to nakedness in the shivering blast; or to the city to ply their needles for eighteen or twenty hours a day, in hunger and cold; or to the street in thousands, spinning yarns and weaving webs that become their shrouds.

'3. It has broken up and destroyed our whole system of working in wood and iron and leather in small shops of one, two, or it may be half a dozen workmen, in every town, village, or hamlet in the country, with blacksmith shops in near neighbourhood upon every road, where every man was a workman who could take the rough iron or unshaped wood and uncut leather and carry it through all its operations, until a thoroughly finished article was produced, and has compelled all to production in large shops, where machinery has minutely divided all work, requiring only knowledge and strength enough to attend a machine that will heel shoes, or cut nails, or card wool, or spin yarn, or do some other small fraction of a complete whole.

'4. It has broken up and destroyed our whole

system of individual and independent action in production and manufacture, whereby any man who possessed a trade by his own hands could at once make that trade his support and means of advancement, free of control by any other man, and has compelled all working men and women to a system of communal work, where, in hundreds and thousands, they are forced to labour with no other interest in the work than is granted to them in the wages paid for so much toil; with no voice, no right, no interest in the product of their hands and brains, but subject to the uncontrolled interest and caprice of those who too often know no other motive than that of avarice.

'5. It has so enormously developed the power of production as to far outstrip man's utmost power of consumption, enabling less than one-half of the producing and working classes, working ten hours a day, to produce vastly more than a market can be found for; filling our granaries, warehouses, depots, and stores with enormous amounts of products of every description, for which there is no sale, though never before offered at such low prices, with multitudes of men and women in the greatest want—being without food, clothing, shelter—without work, and consequently without means to obtain the simplest necessaries of life.

'6. It has thrown out of employment substantially one-half of the working classes. In fact, it has utterly destroyed all regular or constant employment for any considerable class in any industry, and is constantly and steadily displacing able and willing men, and filling their places with women and children; leaving no place to be filled by, and no demand for, the constantly increasing numbers developed in our increase of population, in this way adding to the number of the unemployed. It takes married women in thousands from their maternal cares and duties, and children but little more than infants from the schools, putting them to the care of machinery and its work, until quite one-third of the machine tenders in our country are women and children: thus breaking down the mothers, slaughtering the infants, and giving employment to any who obtain it only upon such conditions of uncertainty, insecurity, competition with the workless, and steady reduction in wages, as create a constant struggle to obtain the little work they do have, and get such compensation for it as will barely support life even when in health.

'These points show clearly the changes which have taken place in all our industries within a period of little more than half a century—changes greater than the world had before known during its whole existence.'

As America is a new country, inhabited by a people of unusual energy and inventiveness, the industrial revolution is running its course there with unexampled rapidity and completeness. But in a general way its effects are the same wherever it is introduced.

Parallel with the development of the industrial revolution there was a revolution of ideas even more important, which also culminated during the eighteenth century, and was the outcome of social and spiritual forces that had long been preparing. Rightly understood, the two revolutions will be found to have a kindred origin. They were both the result of a clearer comprehension and more perfect mastery of nature and of its phenomena and resources. An age which found out the secret of lightning, which drew it from the clouds and made it the messenger of man, naturally enough was marked by the revolt against superstition. For thereby one of the chief strongholds of superstition had been invaded; the marvels of nature were no longer a subject of unreasoning awe, but of scientific inquiry and of application to the service of man. Both revolutions proceeded from the growing knowledge and dominion of man, and a better understanding of his relation to nature and his fellow-men. Hence the triumphs of steam and electricity. The revolt against the 'right divine of kings to govern wrong' took its rise in the same spirit; as also the ideas of enlightenment, humanity, and social progress, which will, we hope, become the common spiritual heritage of mankind.

Such ideas have been largely associated with the French Revolution, but this was really only a terrific explosion resulting from their action on the too fervid temperament of the French. While giving them a world-historic publicity, the French Revolution also tended very powerfully to discredit them and delay their realisation. Even yet the watchwords of the Revolution—Liberty, Equality, and Fraternity—can hardly be mentioned without a cynical smile; and it must be admitted that the contrast between the loftiness of the ideal and the grim realities with which they have been associated in actual history is sufficiently painful.

In their more practical and prosaic form the new ideas grew up and flourished chiefly in Holland and England, especially in England. Greatest of all was the principle of freedom as applied to religion, politics, and economics, and as associated with the right and supremacy of individual reason. It was a far-reaching principle which in the Anglo-Saxon world we claim to have realised in quite a notable way, and undoubtedly it has been a potent sign of progress, though not the universally efficacious means of remedy and renovation that we have believed it to be. In politics many believe that our theory and practice of it are about perfect, and there can be no doubt that in the economic sphere the advance has been marvellous.

In economics the great teacher of freedom was Adam Smith, with whom it was no mere formula, but the well-considered result of wide research into the circumstances of his own and of preceding times, and therefore maintained with constant reference to fact; it was a philosophic principle illustrated, verified, and limited by history. His exposition of the principle was founded on inductive evidence that the true interests of men and nations suffered from industrial and commercial restraints. Many of those restraints had been imposed by the short-sighted and selfish policy of classes and nations. Some of them were simply the survivals of an earlier state of society, at that time necessary and beneficial, but in Smith's time antiquated and worse than useless. It was only natural that when the light of inquiry was turned upon them these restraints should be found to be irrational, vexatious, and oppressive.

Even if the restrictions of which we speak had been required by the best interests of the time before Adam Smith, they would not have been applicable to the new industrial era marked by the introduction of a great mechanical power such as steam. The first effective steam-engine was turned out of the Soho works at Birmingham, in which James Watt was a partner, in 1776, the same year that saw the publication of the 'Wealth of Nations.' Both were products of their time, the result of ideas and forces which had long been growing. For the development of the new mechanical power, which in the course of a few decades was to revolutionise every department of industry, mining, agriculture, manufactures, inland communication and shipping, free scope was the first desideratum. We need not wonder that the principles of Adam Smith were by clear-sighted and progressive men hailed as the true and seasonable word for the new era. What above all things was wanted was room for a mighty development of new forces, to which the old rules were inapplicable, to which obviously no set of rules could be prescribed, room for the energy and sagacity of the founders of English industrialism. It was inevitable that the giant power should break the fetters of the past. The repeal of the Corn Laws in 1846 and the accompanying legislation marked the definite triumph of the revolutionary forces embodied in modern industry.

By many it was thought that the boon of freedom was an effectual means of social regeneration. The naïve confidence of early reformers in the efficacy of liberty is indeed almost pathetic. Relieve industry from its old restraints, and prosperity would set in with a full tide. Release the labourer from his disabilities, leave him free to follow his own interests, and all would be well. Set the negro free and he would at once conduct himself like a Christian gentleman.

Believers in economic freedom were not content with saying that free trade had been one of the conditions of our prosperity; in their view it had been the chief substantive cause of it. Freedom was a social and political panacea. It could work miracles.

Freedom was undoubtedly one of the greatest gains of the new era. Freedom, civil and religious, freedom of thought and speech, freedom to reside where you pleased, and to shape your own career as you pleased—all this meant so much, and was so full of promise. It was a new thing in the history of the world, and, as compared with the restraints of an earlier time, it was a splendid acquisition. Even for the agricultural labourer working for eight shillings a week, or the factory hand drudging for twelve or fifteen hours a day, it was an improvement. Hitherto the change from feudalism had chiefly tended to deprive the English workman of the old securities without conferring on him the blessings of a new era. For him our social system had been oppression and neglect tempered with almsgiving; a *régime* marked by the unholy alliance of oppression and pauperisation. It was well, therefore, to relieve him from the demoralising influence of the old poor-law, and to grant him the right of combination and other rights of a free man.

But even with the gift of freedom the lot of the worker was exceedingly bad. He was landless and uneducated, he had no voice either in local or national government, he had no real guidance or leadership of any kind. Under such conditions had the working man to enter the arena of competitive industry. Such a freedom was in many respects a most cruel mockery.

Yet it was better than the old system, and the beginning of better things.

The sanguine hopes that were founded on freedom as a social panacea proceeded on a false theory of human nature and of the laws of human progress. Real progress can be established only on a wide basis of improved conditions, not through the application of a single formula. Freedom is one of the most important elements in a happy and well-constituted society, but it is only one of many. By itself it is no solution of the real and positive difficulties and necessities of social life. Unless wedded to moral law and resting on a secure economic basis, freedom is not a special blessing. The principle of freedom only means that organisation should be suited and subordinated to the good of man, and not made an instrument of constraint and of suffering. But social organisation and regular terms of union there must be, as we are mutually dependent, and related to each other in a thousand ways.

The doctrine of *laissez-faire* was therefore a well-justified revolt against government in the interests of a ruling class. It had a substantial truth and worth in relation to the selfish, irrational, and antiquated restraints on industry and human freedom. It was the fitting watchword of an era in which, through the industrial revolution and through colonial expansion, such splendid opportunities were offered to enterprise. It has, moreover, a permanent value as an expression of the rights of the individual in reference to society, and of local and provincial interests over against a central government. But it has only too often served as a pretext for shirking social and political difficulties; it has been a confession of the laziness and incapacity of the governors or a sign of the distrust of government on the part of the governed. As we must have government, the rational method surely is to bring it into harmony with the real interests, wishes, and needs of the people.

In any case the history of English industry for the last hundred years must have made it abundantly clear that *laissez-faire* is not the whole truth. It has been the accepted principle among us that government should restrict its activity to national defence, justice, police, and such necessary functions, and that the free energy of the private citizens thus protected by government and from government should do the rest. If government were an unfriendly or doubtful power standing outside of the people, and tolerated only as a necessary evil, such a theory would be reasonable enough. However this may be, it has always broken down in practice. The abuses prevalent in every department of industry that has been given up to unrestricted competition have again and again proved that the theory is not consistent with human well-being. To save the working population of England from moral and physical ruin, government has had to interfere in the most minute details of industrial life, and by an endless series of enactments to restrain the revolting excesses of capitalism. Our theory has been *laissez-faire*; our practice has been individualism under state regulation. The exceptions to the theory have become so numerous that the rule has become the exception and the exception the rule. It is just possible that neither *laissez-faire* nor individualism under state regulation is the right method, but a form of organisation proceeding directly from the needs of the people in harmony with the dominant conditions of social development.

At any rate it is not through the manipulation of barren abstractions or of formulas suited to a past state of things that real progress can be secured. Our economic and political condition is very different from that which prevailed when the historic doctrine of *laissez-faire* was proclaimed.

We have now in a rough and general way sketched the two tendencies which have most powerfully contributed to the formation of modern society. On the one hand is the industrial revolution leading to the concentration of industry in the hands of a limited number of capitalists, and to the divorce of the workers from land and capital. As we have seen, the conditions of the industrial revolution began to establish themselves through the downfall of the mediæval system. It set in with marked intensity towards the end of the eighteenth century, and is still proceeding in almost every country of the world, even the most distant and conservative nations being enveloped by it. On the other hand is the growing love of freedom, and the aspiration after a better life, diffused through all classes in recent times, and especially as connected with the democratic movement. This freer and better life, however, can be realised only under suitable moral and economic conditions.

How reconcile these tendencies at present so largely antagonistic? How can we moralise the industrial revolution, making it subservient to human good? How place the democracy under suitable economic conditions?

Politically the masses of the people form the democracy, but economically they are only proletarians, a landless and even a homeless class. Can we expect that the people which now more and more wield the political power will patiently submit to such an economic position ?

The only satisfactory form of organisation is one that will combine freedom with security, one that will extend and perpetuate the newly-won blessings of freedom, but will add to it the equally necessary boon of security and solidarity, a real and positive basis for a free life ; one that will to freedom wed economic and moral order.

Such is the problem that the Sphinx, which ever waits at the cross-ways of human destiny, now addresses to the nations of the modern world. Upon the answer they give to it will depend their good or bad fortune, perhaps their very existence, in the coming time.

CHAPTER III

EXAMINATION OF THE PRESENT SYSTEM

THE course of social evolution in England has led to the establishment of three great classes—landlords, capitalists, and labourers. Broadly speaking, land belongs to the first class, and capital to the second, while below them is the large third class, which has practically nothing but wage-labour to depend on for subsistence. The produce of the country is in a corresponding manner divided into three heads—rent, profit, and wages—the first going to the landlord, the second to the capitalist, and the third to the labourer; and free competition is the general principle by which the respective shares of the three classes are determined.

As we have seen, this condition of things was gradually established after the downfall of the feudal system and of the Catholic Church, and has especially been developed and consolidated through the mechanical inventions and the triumph of the new system of industry. It is a condition of things which has long dominated and still dominates our entire social system. The economic history of this country is a record of the conflicting interests of the three classes, powerfully modifying and controlling the general history. The struggle of the three for political power is the most important feature of recent history. We may further say that the classical political economy of England is generally an attempt to describe and analyse the economic phenomena that prevail in a country with the above arrangements of land, capital, and labour as regulated by free competition. It accepts the facts and arrangements as established—indeed, it frequently assumes that they belong to the necessary and permanent order of nature—and inquires into the prevailing laws, tendencies, and results of such a system as we have described.

The first of the three classes in our social system are the landlords. Under the feudal system the tenure of land had great public functions associated with it. The feudal lord held the land on condition of performing important social and national duties, especially military defence, and the tillers of the ground had rights which were fixed by custom. In the period that followed the downfall of feudalism the tenure of the landholder was gradually but completely changed. For many generations the landholding class under the king or alongside of him practically ruled the country, and controlled the whole social system in their own interest, with the result that a feudal title was transformed into a private one, and the tenure of land was freed from the public burdens with which it had been associated. From his tenants the landholder exacted a competitive rent. His landowning was no longer a great public function, for which he was directly responsible to the head of the State, but generally a matter of business with many special advantages as a matter of business. In short, the tenure of land had become private, competitive, and commercial.

In all countries the land must be the basis of industry and of the social system. The possession of it therefore confers the greatest possible advantage. But in a small country like England, and at a period of enormous industrial expansion such as we have passed through since 1776, the possession of land carries with it the most exceptional advantages. When the industrial revolution set in, the landowner therefore reaped a golden harvest from the land required for mining, factories, railways, docks, and the dwelling-houses of the new industrial population. The vastly increased demand for food by the same industrial population led to an enormous rise of rents for agricultural land, a rise which was further secured by the imposition of corn laws restricting the importation of foreign grain.

Thus what was once a great national function has been transformed into a department of money-making. Though landowning is also a powerful instrument of social influence and prestige, and is, further, represented by a special branch of the legislature, it is, generally speaking, a commercial matter.

On the whole, the present function of the landowner is not fundamentally different from that of the second class in our social system, the capitalist. The aim and spirit of the landowner is the same as that of the capitalist—to make the greatest possible income out of his property.

The most important member of the present economic order is the capitalist. He is the active and responsible head of the whole system, directing both the productive and distributive operations of industry, at his own risk and for his own profit. After paying to the landlord his charge for the use of the land, after paying his workmen the current wages, he claims as his own the remainder, less or more, as earnings of management, interest of capital invested, and so forth. The present era is the era of the supremacy of the capitalist, the reign of capitalism, in which the capitalist as large farmer, ironmaster, manufacturer, shipowner, merchant, or banker manages industry and substantially controls society. It is true that he shares political power with the landowning and legal class; but, on the whole, he has been too strong even for them, and in economic importance they are far inferior to him. It is to the operations of the industrialist that land has owed its vast increment of value; and it is through the extent and variety of his transactions that the legal class chiefly gain their earnings. The capitalist is the pivot of the whole economic and social order.

Powerful and commanding though the position of the capitalist class be, the case of the individual capitalist is not by any means particularly comfortable or secure. His position generally is one of competition, of struggle on every side of his existence. His relation to the landowner and to the workman has to be determined by competition. He has to compete against rival capitalists, whose business is of a like nature with his own. With these compeers he has to struggle for a share in the market, which may be as wide as the world. The victory remains to the competitor who has most energy, skill, and integrity, or it may be policy and unscrupulousness, who can command the best machinery, the cheapest labour, the cheapest material, the greatest natural resources. In the vast movement of industry there cannot be any plan, any regular proportioning of supply to demand. When we have so many capitalists producing without arrangement with each other and without knowledge of each other's operations, in so many different countries, for a market the needs of which are so imperfectly ascertained, system and order are impossible. The individual capitalist, or firm of capitalists, must take their chance in the open market, which is often as unsteady as the wind. The capitalist is frequently warned of the fact that he has been producing unwisely or too extensively only by the discovery that he can find no sale for his goods, and that he is threatened with ruin. Or he may find that in consequence of the competition of rivals commanding greater advantages, natural or acquired, he can sell only at unremunerative prices. Through the discovery of new methods, through the opening up of new countries with superior resources, through unexpected changes in the public taste and requirements, the heads of an old and valuable industry may find themselves outrivalled. The capitalist, in short, is exposed to all the fluctuations of trade and of prices, to all the capricious movements of a competitive industrial system which is co-extensive with the world. Opponents of the present system are condemned for preaching doctrines of social anarchy; but it may fairly be asked whether our condition is not anarchy already realised.

In the present economic order industrial operations are directed by the capitalist, served by wage-labour.

The characteristic feature of the present industrial order is that the means of production and exchange are owned and directed by a class of capitalists employing wage-labour. The third great class in our social system is the labouring class. Labour is of course an indispensable element in every form of industry. The peculiarity in the position of the labourer under the capitalist system is his prevalent divorce from land and capital, so that he can have access to the instruments of production only by agreement with the capitalist. Only in this way can he utilise his working power and procure the means of subsistence.

Under a system of slavery the labourer also belonged to the owner of the means of production. It was a wrong and cruel system ; but the owner was at least interested in maintaining the value of the human property which he possessed. In the feudal system the serf was attached to the soil, and rendered to his lord a fixed share of its produce and of his labour. Such a system too was deficient in the elements that confer the highest value on human personality. But the serf had a fixed interest in the soil, and he was the owner of the small capital with which he worked. He had to a very large degree a secure economic position, one over which he had a considerable measure of control. Under the present system the labourer has gained freedom but sacrificed security. He has little capital or none, and he has no fixed interest in the soil.

In an age of free exchange the only commodity which the mass of the workers possess is their labouring power, and they have to offer it to the capitalist at whatever price it can bring. To the capitalist it is indispensable, and when labour is scarce the workman can exact favourable terms; but as there is generally a superabundance of labour, the workman is mostly at a disadvantage. The working man, however, has not only to compete against his adult compeers. In the development of industry the labour of women and children has been and still is a powerful rival to his own. Moreover, the invention and improvement of machinery have enabled the capitalist to dispense with labour and resist the demands of the workmen for higher wages and shorter hours. In the great mechanism of industry set in motion and controlled by the capitalist, cheap labour and the best machinery are prime elements of successful competition; and the incessant development of mechanical power is the most effective means of saving labour.

It will now be seen that the cardinal facts in the present social system are these: *first*, the concentration of the means of production in the hands of a limited class, with the corresponding divorce of the workers from land and capital; *second*, a competitive system which must endanger the economic existence of all classes engaged in it, and must under such conditions be waged by the mass of the people on the most disadvantageous terms. It is a system of competition in which one of the competing parties holds the vantage-ground of a virtual monopoly of the natural sources of subsistence and of culture. Such a system must place the mass of the people in a position of economic inferiority and dependence.

Under the present economic order the theory is that the industrial relations of men are controlled by free contract; but the contracts made by the peasant farmer or the labourer with the owners of the soil and of capital cannot be really free. Another part of the prevailing theory is that the general welfare can be best promoted by each man attending to his own; but while believing that this conveys a large measure of truth, especially in view of the abuses of state interference and antiquated social arrangements, we must hold that it is a totally inadequate theory of industry, and assuredly opens the way for a multitude of new abuses.

Most socialists have certainly been too indiscriminate in their denunciation of the principle of competition. Competition is and must always be a potent element of human progress, but it should be conducted on reasonable terms. The principle of competition and generally the principle of self-interest should be subordinated to moral principle. Unfair competition, even when carried on for the prizes of life, is a thing to be absolutely condemned; but the present system is one that exposes to risk the life, character, and happiness of millions of honest and industrious workmen and their families. Unrestricted competition for the necessaries of life, even if conducted on fair and equal terms, must tend to economic and social disorder and insecurity. Waged on such unequal terms, its tendency is towards anarchy aggravated by the oppression and degradation of the masses of mankind.

We consider that such criticism must, in the judgment of all unbiassed men who believe in the supremacy of moral law, be beyond dispute. All who believe that moral principle should govern human affairs and the operations of industry must condemn a social system, the inevitable tendency of which is to place the masses of the people in a position of economic inferiority and insecurity, and to endanger the daily bread of great numbers of the industrious workers. Even the pessimists who despair of the supremacy of high moral principle, but who believe that a reasonable regard for fair play should prevail in the relations of men, must condemn the present system.

Of course, no one will maintain that the evils of society are dependent solely on economic causes, however powerful and prevalent they may be. The economic evils of which we have spoken are at once the symptom, cause, and result of an unsatisfactory state of civilisation. As such they mark an imperfect state of human development, which it should be the aim of all earnest men to supersede by a better and higher. The highest task of all is to indicate the means by which such progress may be attained; but it is very important also to have a clear view of the evils which it is the inherent tendency of the capitalistic system to produce. These evils we shall now proceed to indicate in a more explicit way.

The most conspicuous evil of the system that has prevailed since the fall of feudalism is the degradation and oppression of labour. We may surely regard it as hardly possible for anyone who has not a heart of stone to read the history of English labour without the strongest feelings of indignation and pity! Without land, without education, having no part in local or national government, badly paid, poorly fed, and miserably housed; demoralised by a poor-law system which gave him in the form of alms a wretched portion of that which was his rightful due—such is the historic record of the English workman. In our industrial system he has been subordinated to that production which ought to minister to him. He has had to work long hours of monotonous and demoralising drudgery, which have brought him down to that unblest level of taste and feeling, in which intoxicating liquors have fascinated and brutalised him so fearfully. In our industrial centres the conditions of life and work have been, and still too often are, lurid, depressing, and unfavourable to the development of what is wholesome and refined in taste and character. The workman has had to compete against machinery tended by his own wife and children. In the industrial changes that have so frequently taken place, hundreds of thousands of workmen have been reduced to ruin and exposed to die of hunger or disease brought on by bad and insufficient food and insanitary dwellings. For generations scarcely a voice was raised in his favour. The representatives of law and of the Church passed him by on the other side, leaving him to suffer in his unspeakable misery.

No doubt with trade unions, education, and political reform, a vast improvement has already been made, and we trust there are endless possibilities of good in the continually growing organisation and education of the people. Freedom, education, and organisation will do much for the workman. But the process of reform cannot stop there. These must be made the basis and the means of a further advance. So long as the present wage-system prevails, there can be no real solution of our social difficulties. For many years the trade unions of England have been able tolerably to hold their own in the struggle with adverse economic conditions, but at best they can only secure a working truce and not a permanent peace. The capitalist or combination of capitalists holds the key of the position, and can wait till a sufficient period of idleness has exhausted the resources of the workmen. In times of over-production a few weeks' cessation of work may be a positive advantage to the employer. But whatever the details of the struggle may be, the possessor of land and capital has a permanent superiority, which in the long run will tell against the wage-labourer, and it is a necessity of competition that the capitalist must exercise pressure on his workmen in keeping wages down. This is not the fault of the individual capitalist. He is bound by his position constantly to aim at securing the greatest profit at the least cost. Cheap production is a prime element in successful competition, and one of the chief factors in cheap production is cheap labour. In the intense competition that now prevails in almost every department of industry the margin of profit is extremely small. Every available means that can diminish the cost of production and save the margin of profit must be adopted; hence the inevitable tendency to bring wages down to the lowest practicable level; hence the incessant pressure of the capitalist on his workmen. He must do so. It may be a question of life and death for himself. The employer who keeps wages above the competitive level may risk his own position. The securing of a profit is necessary to the maintenance of the capital without which industrial operations cannot be carried on. Under the present system sufficient profits are necessary for the continuance of industry.

For these reasons the position of the workman under the capitalistic system is necessarily one of dependence and insecurity, tending to oppression, degradation, and impoverishment. Our idea of what is good and right for labour cannot be realised under the existing conditions.

It is only a natural result of the position which the working man has occupied in all past ages of history, and still occupies under the capitalistic system, that the ethical sentiment connected with labour is so fundamentally erroneous. In any reasonable condition of things there should be but one avenue to reward and honour—that of rendering useful service to society. Income should depend on work. Enjoyment should rest on useful service. On all who are not disabled by natural incapacity, sickness, accident, or old age, useful work should be regarded as a natural obligation; and it should be the sole claim to remuneration, recognition, and distinction. If mankind are really to improve, we must insist on the application of such an ethical standard for the testing of our fashionable and prescriptive notions of what is desirable and honourable. We need not say that under such a trial much that is now thought to be a noble vocation would prove to be a trivial and even a criminal abuse of time and means.

Were such a test applied, the workman would have least reason to be ashamed. His task is the most indispensable of all, that of deriving from the earth the means of subsistence and of culture for the entire society. This is an industrial era, and ours is an industrial society, yet even the leader of industry is not reckoned the social equal of the landowner. The most noble and honoured vocation is that of receiver of rents. The remotest association with manual labour is a matter of shame.

In a society corrupted by such a false ideal of duty and honour, we need not wonder that labour should be held in little esteem, that instead of being regarded as a wholesome and honourable activity, it should be shirked as a weariness and degradation. Need we wonder that it should so generally be unintelligent, irksome, and ineffectual? Whereas work should be a willing and happy co-operation of hand, brain, and artistic faculty, carried on in the proud consciousness of a high social function, it is a wearisome drudgery, submitted to as a necessity, borne with reluctance, and flung aside at the earliest opportunity. We have degraded labour, made it monotonous, mechanical, and mean, and yet we complain that its duties are so poorly done.

Perhaps the most painful feature of the working man's lot is the insecurity of his position. During the long periods of depression, work is scarce and precarious, and he must go where he has a chance of finding it. At all times the changes in the labour market are so great and unexpected that he can hardly calculate upon a settled existence. Continual fluctuations of trade force him to move. He has no control, or only a very partial control, over the economic and social conditions under which he must work. A settled home, a piece of land for a garden, a fixed outlook for his family, and a reasonable prospect of a happy and comfortable old age, untroubled by the horror of losing, through want of employment, such savings as he may have made, and of ending his days in a workhouse—these for a large proportion of the workmen in the industrial centres are unattainable blessings. Yet they are unquestionably such as every decent and honourable working man has a right to expect.

Insecurity, however, is a faint word to convey an idea of the dangers which are incurred by large numbers of workmen. There are trades in which they are every day exposed to risk of life and limb, and the wife and mother lives in constant fear of seeing the breadwinner brought home dead or disabled.

This condition of insecurity under the existing system of competition, however, is by no means a special evil of the workman. It is the common lot of all who are involved in it, and not least of the capitalists who are exposed to ruin by it. The conditions of industry are not only beyond the control of the workmen who serve under the capitalistic system. They are beyond the effective control also of the individual capitalists, whose function it is to direct them, so that competition frequently degenerates into disorder, and into an exterminating war carried on with all the weapons permitted by the law, and with many not permitted by law—underselling, bribery, adulteration, fraud, oppression of labour. In times when industry is expanding this may not be so apparent, but when trade becomes dull, stationary, or retrograde, the struggle grows painful, and to many of the competitors disastrous. In this struggle many capitalists are ruined, dragging down with them numbers of workmen who have no control of their economic position, and are helpless under the calamity. Or it may be that a combination of competitors, after crushing or compelling the submission of their rivals, establish a monopoly, and exact from the public an ample compensation for all their expenditure during the struggle. It is a struggle in which the strongest prevail and the weak must look after themselves.

In the United States this process of struggle has gone forward with an intensity which even in this country is hardly known. For obvious reasons industry and money-making occupy a place in America which they cannot command here. Here we have a wider variety of political interests, and culture and society claim a larger share of the national attention. American industry has been engaged in exploiting and dominating a new and immense continent. It has been a struggle between great industrial corporations for possession of a fresh field of enormous natural resources. Never in the history of the world has such an opportunity been offered to a people of such energy, ingenuity, and love of acquisition. Can we wonder that the industrial development is one of extraordinary vastness and diversity, of competition resulting in the ruin of capitalists and workmen, and of combination tending to monopoly, whereby the economic interests of the country are placed under the control of corporations with which purely commercial considerations are supreme?

Under the competitive system the chief aim is to produce things that will sell. In the view of the producer, quality and the effect of his wares on society cannot occupy a sufficiently important place. The inevitable result is the production in immense quantities of commodities of inferior quality, and of many that are positively pernicious and that minister to the worst vices of human nature. How much of very bad alcohol do the nations of Europe, for example, manufacture for the ignorant inhabitants of Africa, and yet they dare to speak of their mission in that continent as the diffusion of Christian civilisation! At home the competitive system is adverse alike to the development of art and to honest work. No doubt adulteration and bad work are to a large degree prevented by the fear of being found out by the intelligent consumer; but there are vast departments of industry where at least the average consumer cannot exercise an effective check, and is exposed on every hand to deception, fraud, and adulteration. The vast expansion of industry has no doubt produced in enormous quantities the appliances of comfort, but how many of them are vitiated by inefficiency, shabbiness, and ugliness! The pride and joy of the true workman in the beauty and thoroughness of his work, how can they prevail against the commercial spirit that now rules the industrial world? The classic example of the depraving influences of *laissez-faire* is London itself with its endless miles of mean and squalid streets, a wilderness of shabby monotony, in which houses are not built for comfort, durableness, or beauty; with its fearful contrasts of wealth ministering to luxury and extravagance, and of the swarming myriads of joyless mediocrity and hopeless misery.

An equally necessary result of the competitive system is the amount of waste prevalent in industrial operations. As there is no regular plan in production or exchange, a vast quantity of wealth is produced which is either not rationally consumed or entirely wasted. This waste of wealth and of industrial power is particularly observable in commercial crises and in commercial wars, whether among capitalists or between capital and labour ; in an excessively numerous class of distributors absorbing excessive profits ; in excessive advertising and display with a view to attracting custom ; in an excessive number of competing canals, railways, and telegraph lines. Ships are built for which there is no employment, and which must therefore lie idle. Vast stores of food co-exist with multitudes of hungry consumers who cannot find work and, not having the means of purchase, must want.

The gigantic development of capitalism has brought new possibilities of waste on the most colossal scale. The noble forests of North America are being cut down to manufacture paper for ignoble books and ignoble journalism. It would appear that the iron ores readily accessible to the most advanced nations of the world, to the British, the Americans, and Germans, are being rapidly depleted. Iron has been the most important material factor in the progress of civilisation. Posterity will not bless us for thus wasting the vast stores which nature has provided for our use.

We have already referred to the insecurity of industrial operations under the competitive system. This is essentially connected with the speculative character of competitive business. As production is so often carried on for a market of unknown and incalculable extent, and for prices which even if obtained cannot be accurately foreseen, uncertainty must very greatly prevail, and the speculative spirit must powerfully affect the general course of business. This spirit of speculation culminates in the great

Exchanges; disturbs legitimate trade; and not infrequently throws into insecurity, panic, and disorder the industrial operations of the country, sometimes of the civilised world.

In the history of the capitalistic system nothing is so extraordinary as the rapid development of mechanical power. It is only natural, when the prizes of success are so enormous and the penalties of failure so severe, that human ingenuity and energy should be wonderfully quickened. The competitive system has indeed brought out a spirit of inventiveness, a readiness of resource, an elasticity and a power of dominating nature which the world has never before seen; and it has called forth a productive and industrial power which to former ages would have seemed absolutely incredible. This development of industrial power still continues, not only in England but in every country where the modern methods have been introduced. But there are two most serious evils connected with it. The productive power tends vastly to exceed the purchasing power and even the needs of the consumers. As the development of machinery and of all the appliances of industry under the competitive system so greatly exceeds the requirements, an immense amount of them are idle or not profitably employed, and industry is threatened with confusion and stagnation. Still worse, however, is the fact that labour, which is one of the greatest factors of production, is thrown out of employment through this excessive development of machinery. But as the labourers form the bulk of the population, and should be by far the largest purchasers, the very force which tends to over-fill the markets tends also to restrict the purchasing power of the majority of the community. Thus industry under the competitive system runs, and must run, in a vicious circle. The peculiar vice of the system is that the development of machinery cannot be duly subordinated to the good of man. It is the private property of a class, and is utilised for the benefit of a class. Every new invention is a fresh disturbance of industry, through the abuse of that which was a fresh triumph of human ingenuity and should have been a blessing to the human race.

All the phenomena of competitive anarchy find their worst development in the great commercial and industrial crises which continually recur, and which have sometimes threatened to become not only universal but chronic. At such times it has been our lot to suffer from world-wide depression marked by features of the most extraordinary character; abundant harvests such as this planet has never seen; a productive power in machinery and skilled labour which surpasses all that the wildest romance has fabled; a large volume of actual production, but with prices reduced so low by world-wide competition that the producer can scarcely make a profit, whilst the consumer is little benefited owing to the large profits pocketed by the middleman. In the midst of all this gigantic productiveness and superfluity, millions unemployed and living within sight of starvation. Truly a marvellous consummation! To this pass have we come under the existing *régime* of private competitive capital. We have voted for individual freedom, and behold we have chaos! Like the magician, we have evoked for our service a mighty mechanical power, but we know not the secret for controlling its labours, and we suffer from its restless superhuman activity.

It is unnecessary to recount the familiar phenomena of an industrial crisis. We have a multitude of competing capitalists of every class, with a market it may be wide as the world. Each has a vague prospect of vast possibilities of gain before him, and when trade is favourable each is anxious to make the most of his opportunities. Machinery is improved, establishments are enlarged and better organised, production grows lively, vigorous, and rapid in an ever-increasing ratio till it becomes an impetuous and feverish rush. Before long the over-filled markets are unable to take off the enormous supply. Goods will not sell. Embarrassments set in, followed by forced sales at any price. Inflation and over-confidence give place to insecurity and panic. Then comes the crash, resulting in ruin to thousands of capitalists and in wide-spread depression and stagnation. Hundreds of thousands of workmen are thrown out of employment. All the classes that depend on the operations of capital, that is to say, the entire society, suffer more or less from the prevailing depression. And we have the fearful spectacle of starving multitudes in the midst of overflowing markets and storehouses; superabundant food and clothing and all the other means of subsistence, comfort and culture, but inaccessible even to those who are most anxious to work; vast numbers of men ruined through the very effectiveness and perfection of the productive forces which they have themselves created. The workers starve because they have produced too much and too well; through the action of mechanical forces which have been created, but are not duly controlled, by man.

So long as these productive forces are wielded in such a chaotic way by private capitalists competing for a world-market, without adequate knowledge of its needs, without arrangement with each other, without system and prevision, so long must such disorder last. The capitalist too suffers fearfully, but it is the workman that must usually bear the heaviest burden of privation and wretchedness.

It would be useful and interesting if we could have statistics of the waste caused by a great commercial crisis ; machinery, shipping, industrial establishments idle and deteriorating in value ; absolute waste in raw material ; food and clothing damaged ; workmen pining away in misery for want of employment, and thus grievously weakened both in character and physique, a fearful loss to their industrial capacity and efficiency.

In recent times nothing is so striking as the growing intensity of international competition. In the labour market the Belgian, Italian, and German with a lower standard of living have competed heavily against the French workman in his own industrial centres. The foreigner has the same effect in the East end of London. The Irish workman has long tended to lower wages in the English labour market. Constant immigration of immense numbers of workmen from almost every European country must eventually bring the wages of American labour down to something like the European level. In the United States and in Australia, Chinese labour has been a menace to white labour. It is not very pleasant to contemplate this aspect of international competition ; the labour which is accustomed to the lowest standard of living is the fittest to prevail under the existing system!

The enormous immigration of cheap labour into America is tending to another serious result, which the people of this country would do well to consider. In international competition success depends on the industrial condition and capacity of the people and on the natural resources of the country. With a rich soil of boundless extent America has long been exercising a severe pressure on the agriculture of Western Europe. In all probability she will become a powerful, it may be a too powerful, competitor in other departments. Some of our industries have already been threatened. During the years to come we shall most probably have to note the growing prevalence of American competition in the various markets. The Americans can produce every variety of raw material in the greatest abundance; no nation surpasses them in invention and in the development of machinery; they have enormous supplies of motive power in coal, natural gas, and water-power. All that they want for successful competition with Europe in the world-markets is a sufficient supply of cheap labour, and this they are now obtaining.

With regard to the growing competition of Germany and Belgium, especially the former, it is unnecessary to speak. The Germans are better educated than we are in languages and generally in matters industrial and technical: and accustomed to a cheaper style of living. Their training has been hardier and more bracing; they have not yet been enervated by excessive prosperity. Such men are dangerous rivals. Not many years ago the supremacy of England in the world-markets was undisputed. Our enormous advantages, both natural and historical, had given us a most exceptional position in industry, so that in the competitive struggle we were easy victors. Now, however, we have to contend against able and energetic rivals with a hardier muscle and a better-trained intelligence than our own. A struggle resulting in a sure victory is a very different thing from one in which the issue in many departments is doubtful, in some is certain defeat.

One inevitable result of the vast increase of productive power all over the world, and of the growing intensity of international competition, is a tendency to the reduction of prices, involving a reduction of profits. Cheapness is the prime condition of successful competition. In itself it is a sufficiently desirable thing. Only it means suffering and, it may be, ruin to the competitors who are less favourably placed. Sooner or later the conviction will be forced upon us that a state of industrial war cannot be favourable to human happiness, even though it do tend to cheapness. After all, cheapness of commodities is only one of the conditions of well-being.

Thus the evils of the competitive system are felt throughout the whole of society, resulting too generally in demoralisation and insecurity, and indeed endangering the very foundation of the social fabric. It tends to divide society into two opposing classes, one composed of the rich and luxurious, and another class of proletarians, thus establishing a divergence of interests which must make for disunion and even revolution.

Though carried on in the name of freedom, the industrial revolution has resulted in the formation of a new wealthy class which allies itself to the old landed class, a plutocracy joining itself to the old aristocracy. It is the two that now govern England, and will to all appearance continue to govern it for many a long year. But they are confronted with an enormous mass of voters without property, who will be a ready seed-bed for innovating principles. A community thus divided cannot be said to have solved the problem of social order.

Even the most important members of the social body are affected by the supremacy of capitalism and of the money-making spirit. Parliament, Law, the Church, and Universities are institutions which exist in order to render service to society, but have too often and too much become dependent upon wealth, are influenced by mercenary considerations, and have made themselves subservient to a class. They have been infected with the spirit of monopoly, living for themselves and consulting their own profit, ease, and comfort, instead of promoting the higher interests of the society which they are bound to serve. Thus the mercenary spirit, which is one of the worst characteristics of the present age, has invaded and perverted Parliament and the Press, and the institutions dedicated to religion and justice, to science and research. Even the institution of marriage, once accounted sacred and sacramental, is largely mercenary. In how many marriages is wealth the decisive element, rather than suitable age and kindred disposition! Nor must we forget the evil effect of the system on the family and the home of the working classes; the overwork of the married women and children in the factories and mines; the unfixedness of the conditions of labour, rendering a comfortable and settled home an impossibility for vast numbers of the working people; the demoralisation and degradation of so much of their life, due not chiefly to intemperance (which is often only a symptom of wider and deeper mischief), but generally to the insanitary, hopeless, and unsteadying conditions under which they must live. The British proletariat are a landless and to a large degree a homeless class. Socialism is sometimes accused of hostility to marriage and the family. But what shall we say of the present system? Who will say that the present state of the family and of the home deserves our approval? Both are too mercenary and nomadic.

It is not too much to say that the prevailing system has perverted our moral judgments and debased our moral ideas. To get on is the accepted rule of life, which is followed with a persistence and energy truly astonishing, and with an indifference to the means of success that is most deplorable. Under the depraving influence of such a system the higher meaning of life is forgotten.

Further, we must refer to the often hurtful influence of the commercial spirit in affairs of government. In the past and to this day rulers have been too much engrossed with wars, squabbling diplomacies and intrigues, with the idle ceremonial of courts, with society and fashionable life. Under the old dynasties the national strength was consumed in dynastic wars, with which the true interests of the people were very little concerned. How much of European history is taken up with the conflicts of Hapsburg and Bourbon! More recently mere class interests and struggles have absorbed a most disproportionate amount of the attention of rulers. In the era of capitalism, commercial wars have taken the place of the old dynastic contests waged during the absolutist period of European history. Under the competitive system the great aim is to extend our markets, to open up new outlets for our manufactures. It is a necessity of the position, and, under the pressure of it, reasons both of morality and of sound statesmanship must only too often be set aside. Are our commercial wars really much better than the old ones? How shall we choose between the Seven Years' War of France against Frederick the Great, which was fought to avenge an epigram of the too witty monarch on the Pompadour, mistress of Louis XV., and the opium war of Britain against China? Vile, both of them. For many years the leading nations of Europe have been eagerly seeking new markets by founding colonies and by annexation in Africa, Eastern Asia, and in the Pacific, in all the unoccupied portions of the world, with little regard to the rights of the natives, and at the serious risk of a general war among themselves. In the same spirit Britain is always adding to her dominions. Is it really a rational policy to endanger the empire by so immoderately extending its boundaries?

Let it also be noted that the same commercial spirit, which continually clamours for the extension of our markets and the consequent enlargement of the empire, has too often grudged the increasing expense necessary for its defence. We cannot afford to pursue a wise and far-seeing policy; our aim has been to run a great empire on the cheap. No rational lover of his country can contemplate the incessant extension of our dominions and the enormous growth of our wealth without a feeling of alarm. We are being ever brought into closer proximity to powerful rivals, to whom our wealth and possessions must be a continual temptation. In our Indian empire, for example, we now touch China on the one hand, and on the other are practically conterminous with Russia. Our occupation of Egypt was for a long time an occasion of quarrel with France. At present, indeed, we are on friendly relations with the yellow races—but who can count on their permanence? A few years ago no great power could approach India except by sea. The situation is very different now. Everywhere we see an extending empire with vast material resources, but with inadequate means of defence; enormous wealth and a declining military spirit. A great empire and a mean and narrow spirit of commercialism go ill together.

A most natural result of the present system is the enormous development in modern societies of the parasitic class. Wherever there is a rank growth of excessive wealth, of idleness and luxury, there all manner of unclean and questionable things grow and multiply. The social parasite may generally be described as one who lives on the social body, drawing his sustenance therefrom, without rendering any equivalent service, without doing any good and useful work. In the view of ethical and social science it matters not essentially whether the parasite belong to the upper or lower ranks of the present body politic, whether he draw from it half a million pounds per annum or extract from it a miserable tribute of ten shillings a week, the accumulated earnings of beggary or infamy. The difference is one of degree only. For there is a wonderful hierarchy in the parasite class, and each great parasite may have hundreds of dependants that prey upon him continually, while these again may have to afford subsistence to a lower grade. But they are parasites, all of them, that live on society without doing any useful work. We must insist on the fundamental principle that income should depend on work of an honest and useful kind, and judge all ranks and professions accordingly. For the scientific student of society, the fashionable and prescriptive standard has no special claim to be considered, except as a peculiarly interesting subject of analysis and of fair impartial appreciation. For him the Apostolic precept must hold good as an inexorable first principle—'If any will not work neither shall he eat.'

In insisting on work or service as fundamental, it will be clear that we posit no narrow conception of usefulness. The true spiritual teacher, the man of science, the medical man or statesman, as well as the true captain of industry and the ordinary workman, all perform a valuable and useful function for the society in which they live. The reasonable needs of a highly organised community are many and various, and we should encourage the development of the capacity required to meet them. But such development ought to be strictly controlled by considerations of social health and social morality. The debasement is awful when skill, capacity, and genius make themselves subservient to fashionable vice.

The growth of parasitism is a marked feature of all old societies; but, as we have said, it is specially fostered by the excessive accumulation of wealth so prevalent in our time. The sons of those who have achieved eminent success in the struggle for riches, finding themselves under no necessity of exertion for a livelihood, and seeing the highest place in the fashionable world accorded to wealth dissociated from industry, naturally pass over to the ranks of the wealthy unemployed. As a natural accompaniment to these great parasites, we have another class of parasites, consisting of hangers-on, toadies, tuft-hunters, and all manner of flatterers and caterers of pleasure, prominent among whom is the *demi-monde*, that most peculiar product of civilisation. And at the lower end of the scale is the ignoble army of vagabondage, largely mixed up with and reinforced from the classes above described. She that began the lamentable career of parasite as the mistress of the rich man ends it as an outcast on the streets, demoralised, drunken, and despairing.

The successive stages in the development of history have been marked by the prominence of certain races. The Greek and Roman had the chief function in the ancient world. The Arab, the Moor, and the Turk have been the great champions of Mahometanism. France was the most brilliant representative of chivalry, scholasticism, and the mediæval spirit. The Jew is in many lands the foremost and ablest promoter of capitalism; but without a rival in the extent and activity of his influence under the existing system is the Anglo-Saxon in England, America, and the Colonies. It is no unimportant part of the criticism of capital to take account of the great race which is its leading representative.

The doings of the Anglo-Saxon as the head of the modern economic system are, indeed, a subject of unspeakable interest to the philosophic observer. His energy, adaptiveness, and still more his power of dominating nature and adapting it to his needs, are such as the world has never seen on so grand a scale. Alike in the strong assertion of individual freedom and in the faculty of colossal organisation he has not an equal.

But in the career of the Anglo-Saxon there are contrasts which, as material either for satire or comedy, are not less extraordinary. The Anglo-Saxon is a race that professes a peculiar loyalty for a religion which most strongly inculcates peace, self-denial, and the spirit of poverty. While in many Continental countries the mass of the people have fallen away from the orthodox Christianity of the creeds and confessions, and even of the Bible, the English-speaking people all over the world render a special allegiance to the old forms of belief. Self-abnegation, the contempt for wealth and for the things of the world are therefore the religious duty of the Anglo-Saxon. Such are his principles. What a contrast to his practice! The acquisitiveness of the Anglo-Saxon has become world-historic. His colonies cover about one-fourth of the land surface of the globe. His commercial emporiums and naval stations are found on every coast. His ships cover the most distant seas. Where our civilisation does not ruin and extirpate the natives in the many lands which we have occupied, we make them the instruments of our enrichment. As the sun pursues his daily course round the world, he sees everywhere some worthy monument of the self-denial of Englishmen. To most honest and respectable Englishmen the only conceivable end in life is to make money, to get on. Every Sunday, in his softly cushioned and luxurious pew, the Anglo-Saxon millionaire listens with perfect equanimity to scriptural lessons of abnegation and to scriptural denunciations of wealth, and on Monday morning hurries forth to increase his store.

And yet we are not content. After swallowing so many of the most desirable countries of the globe, we are ready for more. Every year or so we round off our possessions by incorporating a territory larger than the British Isles. Lately we have seated ourselves in the valley of the Nile, have annexed Burma, a large portion of New Guinea, and have advanced our frontier in South Africa till we can hardly tell where our dominion ends. At the same time we can hardly comprehend how any other nation has a right to share in this gigantic appropriation of the globe. We ruined the colonial empire of France; we effectually curtailed the colonial empire of Holland; we assisted the Spanish colonies in their great revolt. And when the French were recently anxious to acquire a remnant of the spoil, we felt unbounded surprise at the aggressive spirit of our neighbours and their egregious folly in devoting a small fraction of their resources to the extension of their colonial possessions. We had some difficulty in perceiving that the new German Empire might desire a few crumbs of colonising enterprise; and in Central Asia we confront the Russian power, astonished the while at the persistence and unscrupulousness of its advance, as if our experience gave us no hint for understanding such lust of conquest. For be it remembered that as moral teacher and censor of nations England is also pre-eminent.

In a word, if you wish to see a monument of the Christian self-denial of the Anglo-Saxon, look around on his colonial empire and his world-wide commerce. Surely no race ever took such pains to raise a memorial of its contempt for the world, and so worthily succeeded.

Of course it is not implied that the Anglo-Saxon is worse than other nations have been in similar circumstances. The record of Spain as a colonising and conquering power is certainly very much darker than that of England. The doings of the Anglo-Saxon are only such as might be expected of average human nature under the influence of two conflicting theories of life, of Christianity on the one hand, and on the other of the much more prevalent and generally accepted gospel of getting on.

Now, as ever, the selfish struggle for wealth and power must end sooner or later in social disaster, even for those who achieve its most brilliant triumphs. As it was in ancient civilisation, so it is and ever will be in ours. No triumph in history could be more complete than that of ancient Rome, but the season of consummated victory was for those who won it the beginning of ruin. Ancient Rome consolidated under her empire and absorbed the whole civilisation of the old world, Italian, Greek, and Phœnician. After beating down the enemies of the Republic, the Roman nobles threw themselves on the spoils of the conquered provinces. They had at their absolute disposal the products of all the lands and seas of the known world; but in the course of the struggle they had awakened a demon of acquisition and aggrandisement and a burning thirst for spoliation and enjoyment, which could not be appeased even by the colossal plunder of entire civilisations. They quarrelled about the division of the spoil; after devouring all lands they proceeded to devour one another, and such rapacity had a fitting reward. The end was civil war and ruin, the breaking up of one of the strongest social organisations the world has ever seen, followed by universal confusion and catastrophe, till they were glad to seek the peace of desolation under the Cæsars.

In the latter days of the Roman Republic it was a process of mutual destruction ending in the supremacy of the Cæsars. The same process of mutual destruction, the Wars of the Roses, closed the Feudal period in England, and prepared the way for the stern rule of the Tudors. Are we to see a similar process in the capitalist world under forms suited to the new time?

The capitalists and exploiters of the new industrial era have had laid at their feet the spoils of a world vastly richer and more extensive than that of Rome. In the acquisition as in the enjoyment of this enormous wealth we have seen too much of the same egotism and unscrupulousness disguised under the milder forms of the present day. Will the like excesses have a similar consummation? Will the struggles of the capitalistic world terminate in a new Cæsarism, a social Cæsarism resting on the democracy and ruling under democratic forms?

The result will depend essentially on the amount of social virtue we have available to repress the excesses of individualism that have ruined other communities. It will depend on how much we have of the salt which preserves societies from decomposition.

With regard to the great member of the Anglo-Saxon family of nations established on the other side of the Atlantic, we can but say that mere change in the development of political forms will not preserve it from such evils as have afflicted the old societies. In crossing the ocean the colonists left behind them the monarchy and aristocracy and many other social forms hoary with venerable abuse; but they carried with them an institution older and more fundamental than royalty or a hereditary legislature—human nature itself. It was out of human nature developing under well-known historic conditions that the old evils grew; and on the other side of the Atlantic the selfishness, the unscrupulousness, and the mania of acquisition which are so deeply rooted in human nature will, if not repressed, grow rank and bear the usual fruits. Freedom in America seems threatened by the domination of great corporations combining to obtain the control of industrial operations, of governments, and courts of justice. If unchecked by the healthy public opinion and by the collective will of the American people, such corporations may establish an economic, social, and political tyranny quite as oppressive as anything existing in Europe. It will be a miserable thing for the world if triumphant democracy and a material prosperity unexampled in the annals of mankind end in a fiasco such as this. The American republic appears to be on the downward path to the industria land commercial oligarchy which renders a Cæsarism possible.

We have thus briefly indicated the evils necessarily connected with capitalism as first established in England and as now extending over the world. It is hardly necessary to remark that the misery arising from the antagonism of men and classes, and from the oppression of the weak by the strong, did not begin with capitalism. Under older institutions it existed in still worse forms, which in the progress of society were gradually superseded by a better and milder *régime*. Such evils as still prevail under capitalism it must be the aim of the men of progress in present and future times also to remove. It is important to have a clear diagnosis of the disease. The more difficult task is to establish the conditions requisite for a better and healthier development. Of one thing we may be sure, that, change our institutions as we may, there will in this world always be sufficient scope for the reforming zeal and energy of men.

Landlordism and capitalism in England reached their worst in the dark period from 1780 to 1850, their evils being aggravated during the terrible wars of the Revolution and the reaction consequent on the Revolution. Since 1850 especially the evils have been counteracted by many powerful tendencies, some of which we hope are not merely palliatives, but the bright symptoms and beginnings of a better order of things. These tendencies are:

1. Factory and other Acts imposed on the capitalists by the legislature.

2. Increasing organisation of the workmen in trade unions and co-operative societies.

3. The spread of education and general enlightenment among all classes.

4. The growing control of political power by the masses of the people, to whose wishes our statesmen must now give very considerable attention and deference.

5. The vast scope afforded by the Colonies and America for emigration, thus continually relieving the pressure in the labour market at home, and extending the markets for British goods.

6. Moral and Christian influences, which have always tended to check the excesses of capitalism. While we must hold that capitalism is in tendency essentially unfair and oppressive to the workmen, and calculated to create and maintain a dangerous antagonism of classes, there always have been many men who were better than the system under which they lived. Among the capitalists there have been great numbers of kindly, just, and honourable men, who were anxious to do their best for their workers. The prevailing economic system has been one of competition carried on under unjust conditions; but it has been greatly modified by the other influences which have contributed to make the social history of the last hundred years.

CHAPTER IV

WHAT IS SOCIALISM?

One of the greatest difficulties that men have in forming a true estimate of a new social theory is to be found in the limited capacity to realise that there can exist a state of things fundamentally different from our own. In a general way they acknowledge that great changes have occurred in the past, and that the conditions of human life do vary from age to age and in one country as compared with another; but in their political and social judgments they habitually fail to give sufficient weight to such considerations. Only those whose minds are enriched by the study of other countries and widened by the cultivation of the historical imagination can form a reasonable opinion of unfamiliar social conditions.

The past of the world has been at all times so very different from now that no man can adequately picture it to himself. Even the life that men lived not long ago, before the era of railways, of the penny post, and of the daily paper, cannot be faithfully recalled. How much more difficult to revive the still older phases through which our ancestors have passed, even though the imagination be aided by the fact that in remote countries there are tribes which more or less accurately illustrate the backward conditions of humanity.

Instead of being the fixed and normal condition of mankind, the present social system is only one in a long line of succession. Human history is a record of continuous evolution, in which we can see a variety of stages, marked by peculiarities of institution, economic, social, and political. In this evolution the following periods are broadly recognised :

The various forms of uncivilised life, when men were associated in tribes, which at first gained a precarious subsistence by gathering wild fruits, from fishing and the chase ; later on, with the utilising and domesticating of animals, a pastoral life was superadded. At this period land was the common property of the tribe, and the manual labour was done by the women and by slaves. Private property in any form was hardly known.

Then came the agricultural stage, marked by the great change to a settled life in village communities. At this stage land was still generally common property.

In ancient Greece and Rome the village communities grew and were consolidated into the cities so famous in history, the economic basis of which on the whole was slavery. Through the long wars, through the importation of slave-grown corn, and the encroachment of powerful landowners employing slave-labour, the farmers of the early period of Roman history disappeared. In Rome especially the rights of private property were developed in a most rigorous form.

The Roman Empire, which had absorbed the entire ancient world, was overthrown in Western Europe by Teutonic tribes, with whom the agricultural stage passed into the feudal system. The land was held by a feudal tenure, that is, was associated with great public burdens and functions, such as military service. The labour was generally that of serfs. As agriculture was still the only great industry, land had to bear most of the public burdens.

The feudal system, which to people looking back appears a scene of confusion and internal strife, was, as compared with the condition of things that preceded it among the Teutonic nations, really a process of consolidation and building up. Towards the end of the fifteenth century, the feudal states underwent a further process of consolidation into centralised states. The centralised state was represented in England by the personal monarchy of the Tudor period, but it attained to its completest development in the absolute monarchy of Louis XIV. of France. In some great European countries—in Germany, Italy, and Poland—this process of consolidation was arrested or only partially effected. Hence the ruin of Poland, which, after a long period of anarchy, was partitioned by powerful neighbours. After generations of division and foreign invasion, Germany and Italy have only recently attained to national unity. During this period the mercantile system prevailed in economics.

The transformation of the mediæval society resting on feudalism and Catholicism into the modern system was in most countries a long and painful process. The downfall of the feudal system began in England so early as the middle of the fourteenth century; and even yet we are burdened with survivals of it. As regards Europe generally, it is chiefly since the French Revolution of 1789 that the absolute monarchy has been more or less effectively displaced by constitutional government, with parliaments consisting of representatives chosen by the people. In economics the period is marked by private property in land superseding the feudal tenure, by competitive industry and free labour—free competitive individualism. Survivals of an older time are apparent in such institutions as the English House of Lords. The protective system in countries like Germany and the United States has been designed to safeguard their own industries against the competition of other countries. Such an exception, however large, does not affect the general rule. It has only been a detail in the vast system of competitive industry, which is now more or less powerfully operative in every country of the world.

Let it also be said that the changes implied in this vast process of transformation, which has proceeded ever since the origin of human society, have not been artificial or accidental. They have been the outcome and expression of the dominant real and positive tendencies and forces which it is the great function of history to trace and elucidate, especially in their relation to human progress and well-being. Moreover, the economic, social, and political conditions were all of a piece. They were suited to each other, and were all alike the general result produced by the prevailing conditions of social development. Another obvious remark is that the present system of competitive industry, which to most men is so natural and familiar that they cannot even realise the possibility of any other, is but of yesterday. Free private ownership of land, the free right to choose what industry you please, and to follow it as you please, have, even in Western Europe, come into force only since 1789.

Our civilisation is the latest, the most highly developed, the richest in material and technical resources, and it is undoubtedly the most effective for human happiness and culture ever reached by man. At some points we may have been surpassed by ancient Greece, by Italy of the Renaissance, and even by certain forms of mediæval society; but an impartial examination of history will show that these instances were exceptional and very limited in extent and duration. If the enthusiastic admirers of the past could by magic be transported to the times they praise so much, they would, we fear, be grievously disappointed. Our immunity from small-pox and the plague, the result of our superior sanitary methods—how much of the vaunted glory of the older civilisations does it outweigh?

Still the present social and economic order is only the latest stage in a long process of development. Human institutions are not stereotyped things, but passing phases in the process of history. The competitive system can hardly claim to be a permanent or final and complete theory of economic and social organisation. The time must come, if it has not already come, when it will be found inadequate to continue and promote the progress of mankind.

Now it is the contention of socialism that in the evolution of society a period has come requiring the transition into a higher and wider form of organisation, economic, social, and political; a society embodying a nobler ethical ideal, a free democracy with a fit and suitable industrial system; a form of society which will better adapt the mechanical achievements of the industrial revolution to the service of man, for the wider extension of freedom, happiness, and culture. Such a form of industrial organisation, suited to a higher ethical and political stage of human advancement, socialism claims to be.

In the preceding chapter we have seen that the master evils of the present economic system are these two : *first*, the prevalent divorce of the workers from land and capital ; *second*, on this basis a competitive system waged by the mass of the people under the most adverse conditions. It is the tendency of the competitive system to develop and intensify these evils. The more that system prevails over the old forms of industry without check from countervailing influences, the more it tends to accentuate the divorce of the workers from land and capital and to aggravate the mischief due to unfair and excessive competition. The vices of the system are inherent in it. They cannot be cured by any mere palliative or partial reform, but must be removed through a new transforming principle. So long and so far as the present competitive system prevails, it must tend to the degradation of the workers, to social insecurity and disorder.

Our endeavour must be to cure, and, still better, to *prevent* these evils. Such is the problem. How does socialism propose to solve it ?

Socialists maintain that there is only one economic system at once worthy of free intelligent men and compatible with the present industrial conditions. No economic form can be satisfactory which does not terminate the divorce of the workmen from land and capital. But as the inevitable tendency of industry is to assume a large and concentrated form, individual use of land and capital by the mass of the people is no longer a possibility. The only alternative is joint control of land and the large capital worked by associated labour. Whereas industry is at present carried on by private capitalists served by wage-labour, it must in the future be conducted by associated or co-operating workmen jointly owning the means of production. We believe on grounds both of theory and history that this must be accepted as the cardinal principle of socialism. We now proceed to illustrate it, especially by contrast with the leading aspects of the present competitive order.

Under such a system, inasmuch as the working people would themselves own the instruments of production, the present monopoly of capital by a class with all its inevitable consequences would cease. The means and appliances of happiness and culture would no longer be under the control of a privileged minority. Against the evils arising from the practical and virtual monopoly of land and capital by the few, society would protect itself by a system of joint ownership of the means of production; and against the evils of unlimited competition, by the principle of associated labour systematically working for the general good.

Under such a system industry and the welfare of the working millions would no longer be exposed to the risks and anarchy of our competitive system. With associated labour duly organised, with industry systematically arranged for the satisfaction of human wants, the present chaos of conflicting private interests would cease. The triumphs of mechanical invention would no longer be the instruments of private aggrandisement, but would be made directly subservient to human well-being. The happiness and improvement of men in general would be consciously and systematically recognised as the aim and goal of industrial effort. Competition would not by any means entirely cease. It is a principle too profoundly rooted in human nature and too valuable an element in progress to be dispensed with. The aim of the future would be to elevate it to an honourable emulation, a fair and friendly rivalry; there would be special rewards for eminent services to society; the widest recognition of merit would be a possible and desirable thing. It would be a control of society by the best for the good of the whole. There would be competition for social distinctions and rewards, but that competition which places at hazard the daily bread of so many of the industrious people would, socialists hope, be entirely abolished.

Instead of the slave-labour and serf-labour of the past, instead of the dependent and precarious wage-labour of the present, we should have free associated labour, well organised for the general good. Even those who most strenuously deny the possibility of such a system of industry must admit that it is ethically on a far higher plane than the forms which have preceded it.

The fruits of labour would be distributed among the associated workmen according to some good and equitable principle; and each would be free to use his share as he pleased. While land and capital would be under co-operative or collective management, there would be private property in wealth devoted to consumption and enjoyment, in food, clothing, and houses. It is also quite consistent with the theory of socialism that there should be private ownership of land and capital, provided it be under collective and equitable control. An abstract and rigid collectivism, from which private property in land and capital is excluded, appears to be neither desirable nor practicable. A rational socialism is in principle entirely opposed to interference with individual freedom and initiative, so far as they are in harmony with the common good. Its principle is industrial organisation with a view to the free development of men in truth, goodness, and beauty.

The theory of socialism therefore is that the present economic order, in which industry is carried on by private competing capitalists served by wage-labour, must and ought to pass away; and that it will give place to an economic system in which industry will be conducted with a collective capital and by associated labour, with a view to an equitable system of distribution. It means in short that the normal and prevalent form of economic organisation will be one of co-operative industry. It will be a co-operative system perfected and systematised by the experience and progressive activity of men in harmony with the natural laws of social development.

Such, according to socialism, should be the normal or prevalent form of industry. It is a type of economic structure and of social organisation which claims to be the best and fittest under the ethical and industrial conditions that now tend to prevail: and it can prevail only so far as it is best and fittest. If it is the principle of socialism to do violence to the natural order of economic and social development, it can only work mischief, it will be a delusion and a failure, a source of disturbance and suffering. But there is no ground for the assumption that socialism must demand a rigid and arbitrary adherence to the type. As in the old economic orders, slavery, serfdom, and free labour often co-existed, so in any future order there will and should be many varieties of form. If the reasonable historian must admit the insufficiency of the formulas by which he interprets the past, even the hardiest prophet, if he have any reasonableness at all, must confess the weakness of the formulas with which he seeks to forecast the future. But indeed the wisest socialists claim merely to interpret the present, and to show how the dominant forces of to-day inevitably tend towards a concentrated, a collective, and socialised industry. The open eye can see the process realising itself under the widest diversity of tendencies which are continually changing and assuming the most unexpected phases. Whatever the language of agitation may be, thinking socialists are aware that, however precisely they may formulate their theories, the facts will be ground in the mills of history and experience in such wise as no man can foretell. History has never conformed to any formula. Our feudal systems and the like are only a rough and very inadequate expression of a fluent and complex variety of phenomena.

In the past the development of socialism has been most plastic and protean ; and we may expect it to be even more so in the future, in proportion as it is accepted by a wider variety of human beings working under widely various conditions. The development of socialism necessarily follows the development of the large industry and of capitalism, and the large industry is spreading over the world. But should it be found that in certain departments of industry the small production is still the best and fittest, it may continue to prevail there after the co-operative form of organisation may have been introduced into the large and staple branches. Socialism has no quarrel with free and independent labour. Its contention is that wage-labour in the service of competing capitalists is not in harmony with the growing technical, political, and ethical conditions.

Such is the general theory of socialism. But how is such a theory to be realised? On what methods does it rely for the promotion of its ideal?

This question will be discussed in another chapter. For the present we may say that if socialism be realised, the methods of realisation will, like the forms assumed by it, vary indefinitely with the differences of time and country. It is unreasonable to prescribe any definite method by which a great principle clothes itself in fact. But it is maintained that the beginnings of such a social transformation are already discernible. They may particularly be seen in the co-operative movement, which has made such rapid strides in England. Many ardent socialists are disposed to deny that this movement is a realisation of their principles; but, as we think, very unfairly. It grew out of the socialism of Robert Owen and the Christian socialism of Maurice and Kingsley. In the mind of its ablest leaders the conscious purpose of the movement is a peaceful transformation of industry of the kind we have described above. Inspired by the hope for the future which the movement excited in his mind, a sagacious and sympathetic thinker like J. S. Mill declared himself a socialist.

The co-operative movement is rapidly growing in all the progressive countries of the world. It has stood the severest tests of experience and shown the clearest symptoms of a strong and healthy vitality. It is the hope of many that, from the solid basis already gained, the co-operative movement may by just and peaceful methods more and more extend over the domain of industry. The present co-operative system is, of course, only a partial application of the principle of socialism. But great principles are not introduced ready made and complete. They are realised after long preparation, through gradual processes of change, in a multitude of details often prosaic enough, by leavening and transforming the complex mass of facts that make up history.

The socialistic movement will be most likely to attain to a vigorous and durable life if it grow out of the free activity of the people. Probably the best thing the state can do for it is to clear the way for its development by removing antiquated institutions, especially those connected with local government, and with the tenure and transfer of land, the effect of which has been to repress the free initiative of the working people. Through the extension of co-operation, through its application to agriculture and mining, and through the co-operative organisation of trades, after the manner, it may be, of the ancient guilds, but suited to the needs and exigencies of modern industry, the movement might spread without any special furtherance from the state.

While it does not depend for its realisation on the

existing organs of society, socialism may be greatly promoted by them. It may be realised through them. Of these organs there are three leading forms: first, the parish, township, municipality, or commune; second, the county or province; third, the central government or state. In proportion as these forms of government are developed so as to promote the real interests of the people, which is the aim of all true statesmen, the nearer we are to the political conditions required by a rational socialism for its realisation.

Education, post office, telegraphs, lighting and water have all passed or are passing from private to public control; and in many countries railways. Many reasonable people believe that building sites in towns should be under municipal ownership. Thus it is practically acknowledged that there are important matters in which it is expedient to enlarge the sphere of state and municipal control. And when we have restored the self-governing township or parish to full life in the rural districts, a further extension of associated action will be desirable and practicable. In this direction, too, what is most needed is scope for the development of the free energy of the people co-operating for the satisfaction of real needs.

Most critics and some adherents of socialism assume that the theory implies that all those economic changes must be effected by the state, a burden obviously under which the strongest central government would stagger and fall. On the other hand, many socialists look forward to the abolition of the state. All such views are one-sided. Railways and other large organisations would require to be under central management, but the most obvious requirement of the socialistic theory is a vast extension of local association. Instead of being a return to the crude and undeveloped simplicity of barbarism, instead of being a scheme of excessive centralisation and of state despotism, a rational socialism aims at a more highly, a more widely developed social life and organisation—a stronger and more effective central government, with a wider variety of local and subordinate institutions. It is a theory of nobler and wider social forms inspired by a higher ethical spirit, able to wield in the service of man the infinitely elaborate yet delicately simple and effective technical and material civilisation, which has grown up since the application of steam and electricity to mechanical improvement.

Thus the problem could be gradually worked out by a people continually growing in freedom and intelligence, and in the wise adaptation of all its institutions to the wants of the time. In countries that are accustomed to peaceful and constitutional methods of progress, there is no reason why the change should not proceed smoothly, by open discussion, by continual experiment and steady advance along approved lines, with entire deference to law and order, through the progress of enlightened opinion. The innovators would bear the responsibility of showing that their theory of improvement is desirable and practicable. There would be no need for violence or confiscation. As the transformation proceeded, a fair price could be paid for the land and capital transferred to the co-operative system. In the breakdown of capitalism, which the socialistic theory assumes as bound to precede the advent of the new era, the selling price both of land and capital would probably fall. In fact, under American competition our land system has broken down, and the selling price of English land has fallen.

But each country has to work out its destiny in its own way in accordance with its special circumstances and the special character of its people. Whether owing to the temperament and habits of the people, or to the condition of their social and political development, there are countries to which revolution seems more natural than quiet and orderly progress. There are nations that periodically indulge in sensational effects and theatrical situations claiming the astonishment or admiring sympathy of the world. And deplore it as we may, force, violence, and war are potent factors in the real development of mankind.

Nor need it be said that, though each nation must be primarily responsible for its own social development, the whole movement will be international. As in other large movements, one nation will influence another. Great ideas and great movements do not respect narrow geographical boundaries and the conventional limits of states.

Though socialism most naturally allies itself with the advancing democracy, there is no absolute reason why the actual control of the movement should be democratic. In Germany it is quite possible to imagine with Rodbertus that it might proceed from the emperor. It would be the realisation of an idea entertained by Lassalle and to some degree by Bismarck. It is possible that the imperial court and its servants, wearied of compromise with the moneyed middle class, might throw themselves unreservedly on the workers both of town and country, and establish a socialist empire. Such an empire, served by capable officials like the present and supported by a people's army inspired with the enthusiasm of a better social order, might find its strength and stability immeasurably increased. When the time is ripe for it, a policy of this kind might be a wiser and fitter one than the enforced and reluctant deference to the capitalist class. In the dissolution of its feudal system Prussia accomplished, in a few years and far more effectually, a transformation which in England dragged out its painful course for generations. Germany has already made a very substantial beginning in state socialism. Improbable as it may appear to many, we can easily conceive the possibility of circumstances in which a social empire would be not only desirable but necessary.

There can be no doubt that in the struggle among nations, which at least in the immediate future is likely to become more intense than formerly, the people that first brings its social organisation into harmony with the new conditions will have an immense advantage. The country that can first raise its working population to an intelligent and enthusiastic solidarity of feeling and interest, a compact nation of free instructed men, would in the scientific warfare of to-day have an exceptionally strong position against a government of capitalists dragging after them an unwilling, demoralised, and ignorant host of proletarians. It would have all the enthusiasm of the armies of France during the First Revolution, joined to the more perfect technique of the present day. If socialism is the form of economic organisation best fitted to produce such results, it would have to be adopted. In a time of highly organised societies it is the fittest type of organisation that must prevail.

But, whatever the nominal form of government be, it will have to take account of the needs and wishes of the people. Even an imperial or conservative socialism must rest on the democracy. The prevalent political force is the democracy, and with it the socialist movement ever tends to ally itself.

Socialism also most naturally allies itself with an unselfish or altruistic system of ethics. Under a socialistic system the generous and well-endowed aspirant would be invited to find a field for ambition in the service of society. In such a condition of things there would most naturally be provided a nursery for noble, liberal, and unselfish activity.

But we must insist that the claim of the class most deeply interested in the question, the working class, is primarily a demand for justice. As they have to bear the burden of society, they claim a reasonable share in culture and enjoyment. It is not a mere question of sentiment, of humanitarian idealism, of vague philanthropy. It is a solid demand for redress and for a better adjustment of social duties and rewards, supported by the toiling and suffering millions who have for untold generations had little voice or none in the arrangements of society, but who are now beginning to understand the real position of affairs and to organise in defence of their rights.

It is a demand for justice, but we hope that the development of the movement will be attended with a continually growing ethical sentiment in every department of human thought and action. The dominant factor in history will always be the moral one. That the movement may become wiser, more peaceful and unselfish, that there may be an increasing regard for the rights of others, must be the wish of all good men.

We have said that the fundamental principle of socialism is this : associated labour with a joint capital with the view to a more equitable system of distribution. Thus we might define the final aim of socialism to be an equitable system of distributing the fruits of labour ; and economics end where they began, with the consideration of human needs.

With regard to an equitable system of distribution the various theorists have differed greatly, as was natural. A perfectly good and just system of remuneration is not possible in this world. All that we can expect is a tolerable approximation to equity and reasonableness. Adherents of socialism who insist on a theoretically just method, and hypercritical opponents who condemn it for not being able to offer such a method, totally misunderstand the conditions of the problem. Should remuneration be equal ? Should it be according to the reasonable needs of each ? Should the principle of remuneration be one that takes both merit and reasonable needs into account ? Should the workman receive the full product of his labour ? The last is plausible in appearance, but when examined is found to be void of meaning, for in the highly organised industry of the present, which is really a co-operation of the whole working society inheriting the labours of the past, how can we discriminate the individual share of each worker ?

Such questions may and will be discussed ; but theorists should not expect that the world will wait till they have settled them. It is never reasonable to resist an improvement because you have not got what you consider theoretically right. The wise man will always be content with the best attainable good.

It is always well, however, to measure the attainments of the present by a higher standard; and as a general principle we might suggest one that has regard both to merit and needs. But in any case we must remember that in the transition to the future no theorist intends to cast away the experience of the past as a worthless thing. Even the most revolutionary socialists do not propose to construct the world anew. In each step of our progress, whatever it be, we shall need to have regard to the lessons of the past.

In conclusion, we repeat that socialism is a new principle of social organisation based on a new form of industrial organisation. While most naturally associating itself with the new democracy and with an unselfish and humanitarian view of life, its essence is an *economic change*. Everything else is accidental, and in the view of socialism non-essential. Questions connected with it as to religion, ethics, politics, and as to the methods of realising the theory, may be and are of supreme importance; but they are not socialism.

No thinker has stated the socialistic position with greater clearness and insight than John S. Mill in the chapter of his 'Political Economy' on the probable future of the working classes. After examining and commending the system of industrial partnerships, Mill goes on to say, 'The form of association, however, which if mankind continue to improve must be expected in the end to predominate, is not that which can exist between a capitalist as chief and workpeople without a voice in the management, but the association of the labourers themselves on terms of equality, collectively owning the capital with which they carry on their operations, and working under managers elected and removable by themselves.'[1] With his unequalled candour and open-mindedness, his enthusiasm for progress and his great sympathy for the working classes, Mill was remarkably well fitted to appreciate both the good and the objectionable sides of the historic socialism. He was familiar with English socialism; he had followed with deep interest the development of the movement in France from the days of Saint-Simon; and he saw in the co-operative movement of both countries the beginnings of a new era for the labouring classes. On some points one cannot agree with him, as in his strong accentuation of the population question, and his excessive estimate of the value of competition (though on these matters socialists generally go to the other extreme). Yet this chapter on the probable future of the labouring classes still remains the best and wisest account of the spirit and economic aims of socialism. And he accepts for himself its fundamental principle in the following words: 'I agree then with the socialist writers in their conception of the form which industrial operations tend to assume in the advance of improvement; and I entirely share their opinion that the time is ripe for commencing this transformation, and that it should by all just and effectual means be aided and encouraged.'

[1] See Mill's *Political Economy*, People's Edition, p. 465.

CHAPTER V

CURRENT VIEWS ON SOCIALISM

SOCIALISM is a theory of social organisation, based on a new scheme of economic organisation. In its historical development, as we have seen, it has been a most plastic and changeful thing, varying according to the temperament and condition of the people that adopt it, and mixed up with the most contradictory opinions on marriage, religion, ethical and political philosophy. In these circumstances we need not be surprised that inquirers and critics, even when tolerably well informed, have confounded the essence of the movement with its external characteristics and accidental accompaniments.

It is the aim of the present chapter to emphasise and illustrate the fundamental principle of socialism by discriminating it from opinions with which it has so frequently been associated.

1. It is still by many believed that socialism tends to subvert the family and the Christian ideal of marriage. Some of the leading socialist writers have indeed enunciated theories at variance with these institutions. But it should be remembered that such opinions are not peculiar to socialism, and that they have been most strenuously opposed within the socialist schools. As a theory of economic organisation

we cannot see that socialism can have any special teaching adverse to marriage and the family. On the contrary, it should tend to purify and elevate both, by eliminating the mercenary element so common in the marriages of the present day, by relieving the drudgery of women, both indoors and out of doors, and by abolishing prostitution—that vilest plague-spot of the existing society. Its effect should be to promote a more genial form of nurture and education for both sexes, and to make woman the happy and cultured friend and companion of man, and especially so to organise society that marriage should be a life union of man and woman endowed with kindred aims and disposition, and not, as it so often is, a calculated arrangement dictated by convenience, wealth, and social position, in which youth is wedded to decrepitude and beauty to capital. At present, love, marriage, and the family are too much perverted by the mercenary spirit, which it is a chief aim of socialism to repress. To what baneful extent the Christian family has been injured by the employment of women, especially married women, in factories and mines we need not repeat here. The economic reforms and ethical tendencies of socialism should directly and powerfully tend to remove the worst evils connected with the mutual life of men and women.

2. It is also by many believed that socialism is hostile to Christianity and is naturally associated with secularism and a revolutionary materialism. So it frequently is and has been. But the connection of socialism with views of this nature is purely an accident. Socialism has also been associated with Christianity, both Catholic and Protestant. Considered as a

principle and theory of social and economic life, socialism is marked by the entire harmony and even identity of its moral spirit with that of Christianity.

One of the most remarkable features of the last century was the vigorous growth of innovation and revolutionary opinion on almost every subject of human interest. Historically socialism has itself to a large extent sprung up and flourished in such a medium. It is not surprising, therefore, that it has been so much associated both by friends and opponents with new opinions of every kind. And yet the distinction seems clear enough. Socialism is an economic transformation designed in the interests of the poor man, so long oppressed, so long excluded from anything like a fair participation in the best blessings of culture and enjoyment. In England, one of the movements for his emancipation, viz. education, was long delayed through the contentions of the various sections of the Christian Church. Why should his economic emancipation be deferred, why should the struggle for it be confused and obscured by the importation into it of theological and speculative controversies which are foreign to it, and should be fought out in other fields and on their own merits ?

With regard to the prevalence of anti-Christian feeling in socialist schools, it should, moreover, be remembered that socialism has flourished chiefly on the Continent, where the defection of the mass of the people from the creeds and churches is much more pronounced than in this country. Continental socialists are not more anti-Christian than Continental liberals have been. The feeling of antagonism in both is largely due to the fact that the churches of the

Continent have been taken into the service of the state and the ruling classes. The feeling is not so much anti-Christian as anti-clerical, the clergy, the official representatives of the Church, being regarded as the dependent allies of the crown and nobility.

But it may be said that socialism is essentially materialistic, inasmuch as it so strongly insists on earthly happiness. For this too we can see no necessity whatever. Does not the objection rest on a narrow conception both of religion and of socialism? Socialism is simply a means of realising a good and happy life. Such realisation should begin here and now. In this a true and worthy conception of religion entirely agrees with socialism. The kingdom of heaven must begin *on earth* in the heart and conduct of living men. Even to say that, while socialism insists on the external and economic influences for good, religion emphasises the internal, is not altogether accurate. The two cannot be dissociated, and it is the mark of a superficial philosophy to separate them. Man must be treated as a whole. It should be the aim of all true reform to improve him in soul, body, and estate.

3. It is believed by many that socialism aims at an equal division of property. It is not easy to understand the real meaning of those who entertain this strange misconception of the subject. Probably they think that the entire wealth of the community is to be divided into equal parts corresponding to the number of the people, and that each will have his share of it for his private use and possession, and they complacently proceed to refute this imagination of their own by alleging that in twenty-four hours the con-

dition of inequality will have recommenced, and all the old evils will have returned. No socialist contemplates such an absurdity. Socialists propose the concentration of land and capital under social control with the view to an equitable distribution of the fruits of labour. Land and capital, which are the means of production, instead of being divided, are to be put under collective management for the common good. Wealth applied to consumption must of course be divided among the individuals who enjoy it. Socialism does certainly contemplate a fairer division of the fruits of industry.

It is more rational to maintain that socialism aims at a state of equality inconsistent with the facts and possibilities of man's nature and position. With regard to such a contention, however, we must say that any definition or statement about a condition of equality is too vague to be of any real service. Equality is an abstraction surrounded with ambiguities, and reasonable men will be careful how they handle it. Men are not equal either by birth or training in physical, intellectual, and moral qualities, in the power of enjoyment, or in the capacity to work and to dominate the conditions by which life is circumscribed. We cannot even say that men should have equal opportunity for development, culture, and happiness without serious reservation, when we remember that what is the just and full measure of one man's development may be scanty measure for another. In fact, equality is an abstraction calculated only to mislead the average mind. While we believe that the idea contains a substantial, though not easily definable, measure of truth, it only makes confusion worse confounded to bandy it about so freely in political and social controversy.

4. It is sometimes said that socialism is in principle hostile to capital, that socialists are a set of ignorant and misguided enthusiasts, who, wishing to produce without capital, would thus destroy the economic basis of civilisation, and reduce the world to the condition of the primeval wilderness. Such a statement, like some of the preceding, can spring only from ignorance or wilful misrepresentation, or from that confused mixture of both which so frequently passes current in ordinary discussion. Instead of undervaluing or denying the importance of capital, socialists wish to make it more effective for the good of man by transferring it from the private property of a few competing individuals to the systematic management of society. They believe it to be so essential to mankind that it should not be left in private hands, but should be under co-operative control for the common good. Capital is the result of the combined efforts of successive generations of workers; it should be regarded as the collective heritage of the industrial society, and not as the peculiar possession of a comparatively small minority.

Such is the principle of socialists. It may be that their system would not prove so effective for the accumulation, maintenance, and utilisation of capital, that it would be wasted and squandered under social management. That is a rational objection, supported by the late Professor Cairnes, with which socialists must deal. We reserve the consideration of it to a future chapter.

5. Socialists frequently speak of their theory as a

programme of social revolution. It is so in the sense that it implies a vast change or transformation in society. But it is a great error to suppose that it is a revolution in the sense that it has any necessary or special connection with anarchy or violence. There is a socialistic party which inculcates the exercise of force in overturning the existing society, but it is a comparatively small minority, and has been trained or driven to such a method of action in countries where free inquiry and discussion have been mercilessly repressed. While accepting it as a necessity, even they do not approve of a violent policy as an eligible or desirable method of social reform. What socialists have generally desiderated above all things has been untrammelled and unprejudiced inquiry. For the most part they have been men profoundly convinced, all too sanguine, indeed, as to the validity and practicability of their schemes; and, with naïve confidence in the power of truth as they understood it, have been most ready to challenge discussion, and to stand or fall by the result. Their appeal has been from the accepted theories and institutions to science and reason, to the first principles of society and of social progress. This was a marked feature of the early forms of socialism. The school of Saint-Simon claim to have been the first to warn the governments of Europe of the approach of revolutionary socialism—the socialism, that is to say, which resorts to force or insurrection. The violent forms of socialism have flourished chiefly where free discussion and the reasonable right of combination among working men have been prohibited.

For the rest it should be remembered that great

changes in history have generally been accomplished or attended by the exercise of force. This has been due to two great and constant causes. On the one hand, those who were interested in the continuance of the old condition of things have naturally not seen their way to retire from their privileged position, or to give up their vested rights or sacrifice their fixed ideas of duty for the new order, which probably they neither understood nor cared to understand. On the other hand were the hasty and impatient innovators and iconoclasts, the interest or mission or manifest destiny of whom urged them to attack the old order. From these conflicting views inevitably resulted the irreconcilable parties, which have so frequently made human progress the occasion of bloody and implacable war. So it may unhappily be in the social debate and trouble that at present are preparing in so many countries of the world. Even the most peaceful socialists hardly expect that the difficult questions that demand attention can be solved on grounds of pure reason, justice, and humanity; and there can be no doubt that the more resolute of them anticipate a terrible international struggle of classes. If this be so, if it be in the nature of socialism to evoke a great struggle of classes in the future, this is only one imperative reason the more why it should be impartially and accurately studied. It is a most sufficient reason why we should seek to know the causes which have produced it, its real aims and tendencies, and to discover the secret of its strength, so that the collective intelligence of the civilised world may be better able to deal with it. If, as many think, socialism really be a revolutionary monster red with blood and seeking to overthrow altar and family and all that is sacred and precious in human institutions, it is well that the champions of truth and righteousness should know the natural history, the habits and the vulnerable point of the dread beast.

Even in a movement of which the main scope or method is to be condemned there may be valuable subsidiary lessons. Socialism is assuredly one of the most powerful and vital movements of our time, and it cannot be satisfactorily met by unsympathetic condemnation and repression. Resting as it does on widely prevalent discontent among the workmen of many countries, it can be well and duly treated only by the intelligent, energetic, and sympathetic action of many minds anxious to promote the well-being of men in harmony with the fundamental principles of human nature and of social progress.

But it may reasonably be said that it is the aim of socialism to make revolutions a thing of the past; to establish such a real harmony of interests by removing the present causes of contention among classes and nations that the conditions tending to violent change would be eliminated. Political thinkers maintain that extreme democracy, in the United States for example, is the most stable form of government, inasmuch as political change has reached its final stage of development. No further extension of popular rights being possible, the political development is complete. Such disturbance as is caused by reforms or efforts after reform in old societies is by the very nature of the case excluded. Premising that in this world of change such finality can be final only within the present horizon of social development, should we not say the same of socialism ?

After all, be it remembered that revolutions are not an invention of socialism, as some of its critics would almost appear to suggest. If in many respects the most undesirable, revolutions are also the oldest phenomena in the history of society. Many of the systems which now so complacently object to socialism as revolutionary, were themselves revolutionary almost the other day. A few years ago Liberalism was revolutionary in many European countries; is even yet new and unsettled in some of them. For more than a century and a half the Protestant Reformation was the cause or occasion of civil and international upheaval and bloodshed. To go further back, there was no doubt a time when the culture of wheat and the use of the plough were a revolution in social economy, which the grey fathers of the prehistoric dawn of the world reprobated, as an irreverent departure from the old paths, in such imperfect utterance as was then available. And it may be that the originators of such useful industry were persecuted or driven out of the primeval tribe before a grateful posterity raised them to the rank of gods and demigods as the benefactors of mankind.

But in our country, happily, this discussion is an idle one. We have long enjoyed the right of free inquiry; and there is growing scope for free effort in social and economic organisation. If the co-operative type of industry is the best and fittest, we have opportunity for bringing it to perfection and for putting it to the test both of criticism and experience. If our social conditions are sound and healthy, violent innovation will find no leverage by which to disturb them. If they are not sound and healthy, a government which must follow the progress of opinion cannot repress change. In this country we are agreed that the final appeal must be to the collective will and opinion as formed by experience and free discussion.

The views of socialism hitherto considered in this chapter have no necessary connection whatever with the fundamental principles of the subject. They have been associated with it in the course of its development, but are not part of its essence.

In the remaining pages of the chapter we shall discuss theories and definitions of the subject, which, though inadequate, have at least a substantial measure of truth.

In our first chapter we spoke of socialism as the *cause of the poor man*, as a social transformation designed in the interest of the poor. The same idea appears in the definition of socialism as the *economic philosophy of the suffering classes*, or the struggle for the emancipation of labour. It is probable enough that this will ultimately be found to represent the historical meaning and import of the movement; that socialism will be accepted as a general name for a series of struggles, the aim and tendency of which are to accomplish the economic and social deliverance of the working classes. At the very least we can at present say that such definitions throw a large and real light on the whole subject. In the front of every socialistic programme stands the question of the emancipation of the labourer, the amelioration of the lot of the poor man, and his full participation in the material, intellectual, and spiritual heritage of the human race.

It would be both premature and one-sided, however, to identify socialism with such great and comprehensive issues. Indeed, they are both too wide and too narrow. Socialism can by no means claim exclusively to represent the cause of the poor man. It is a mistake too often made by socialists to assume that they hold a monopoly of good will and sympathy for the workman. In this country especially socialism has simply been a phase, and not a large or influential one, of a general movement on behalf of the suffering classes. The field has been a wide one, in which statesmen, philanthropists, and good men of very different ways of thought have zealously laboured according to the light that was vouchsafed them. In political reform since 1832, in education, the temperance cause, the diffusion of the products of the cheap press, in factory legislation, and many other movements, we see the beneficent action of men who had no part in socialism, but who earnestly desired the welfare of the poor and suffering. It is true that the sympathy of many has been half-hearted, wanting in insight, in comprehensive and resolute purpose. Many of the schemes of reform are only palliatives, not remedies; excellent as preparatory and subsidiary to a wider scheme of transformation, but not to be mistaken for the scheme itself. It may be that socialism will eventually absorb all the other forces and movements concerned in the emancipation of labour, but it has not yet done so; and if ever it do, it will only be by proving the truth and righteousness, the practicability and desirability of its theory.

But considered as a definition of socialism these phrases are also of too narrow a scope. For socialism professes to act not only in the interest of the poor man and worker, but of the small capitalist crushed by the competition of the larger, and in the interest also of the great capitalist himself, whose ascendency is continually threatened by the fluctuations of trade, and the rivalry of his powerful compeers. It will assuredly be for the true good of the wealthy and luxurious idler, pursued by a devouring *ennui*, to whose existence a moderate share of honest work would give rational meaning and a wholesome stimulus. For the parasites of every class it would be a saving deliverance from a base and harmful life. In short, the aim of socialism is to establish a real solidarity of interests, to render possible for all men a healthier and happier life by a more general distribution of labour and its rewards.

We may add that the question of the poor is not a new phenomenon in the history of the world. It is about as old as human society itself, and has recurred under various conditions with various efforts towards solution in all countries and in all generations. It was a burning question in the cities of the ancient world; it led to the peasant wars of the Middle Ages. In many countries and for many generations, indeed, the poor labourer could hardly move under the superincumbent weight of misery and oppression. He could not speak for himself. The high annals of history have hardly a word to spare for him and his concerns. But the seeing eye can discern his sad estate. The hearing ear can hear the moaning of labour overtaxed, the sobbing of heavy-laden women, and the wail of children crying in vain for bread. This problem has now appeared in a form entirely new, induced by the novel conditions of industry peculiar to our time. Socialism is the most thorough and comprehensive expression and proffered solution of the problem thus reappearing under strange conditions. But it is more than this. It claims to be the fittest scheme for the reorganisation of society as a whole.

In this connection we may refer for a moment to the claim of socialism to be the *economics of democracy*; to be the only economic system consistent with a stable and well-constituted democracy under the existing conditions. If so, its claim to dominate the future is assured; for nothing can be more certain during the future of which we have any knowledge, or which has any interest for us, than the predominance of democracy in the world. This, indeed, is the Gordian knot of the entire social problem all over the world—What *is* the economic form suitable to the modern democracy? But the question must not be begged under cover of a definition. Such a claim on the part of socialism must be tested by argument and, above all, by experience. As we are now only defining the scope and tendency of socialism, all we can do here is to register the claim and refer it for discussion to a subsequent chapter.

Socialism is very generally understood to mean *systematic interference of the state in favour of the suffering classes*, the use of the public resources on behalf of the poor. This view of the subject receives countenance, at least, from Laveleye, who defines socialism thus: 'In the first place, every socialistic doctrine aims at introducing greater equality in social conditions, and, in the second place, at realising those reforms by the law or the state.' According to this theory of the matter, it must be the aim of all socialistic agitation to gain control of the state, and thus bring about a reform or revolution in the interest of the working classes. In accordance with a view that regards all special action on behalf of the poor as socialistic, the English poor-law and the social legislation of Bismarck must be so described. The radical socialism of men like Clemenceau and Chamberlain must be referred to the same category.

There can be no doubt that a government which systematically endeavours to correct the inequalities handed down from the past, and which seeks to bridge the gulf between rich and poor by wise and sympathetic legislation, should be esteemed as socialistic in tendency. The growth of such a tendency in government is certainly one of the most significant signs of the time. But it is most misleading to identify the socialistic movement with state or legislative action. The state is merely the central organ of society, important and most powerful, no doubt, but subject to every kind of modification from the prevailing character of social development.

In its most comprehensive interpretation socialism is a theory according to which society, in its various forms and through its various organs, should own the means of production and manage industry for the general good. Socialism is a new type of social and economic organisation, the aim and tendency of which are to reform the existing society, the state included. It is a principle of social change, which goes beyond and behind the existing state, which will modify the state, but does not depend upon it for its realisation.

The attitude of the historic socialism to the state has varied greatly. The early socialists were ready to accept help from any quarter, but in the experiments in association which they attempted they depended on private enterprise. Louis Blanc and Lassalle invoked the aid of the democratic state. The aim of the Marx socialism is to supersede the existing states by an international combination of workmen, and eventually to abolish government as we understand it. The fundamental principle of Anarchism is the abolition of government. In fact, the general attitude of the organised socialists of the present day towards the state is one of distrust and hostility. They regard it as an organisation for exploiting the working classes and maintaining them in economic subjection. In the English parliament the representatives of labour are few in number, and socialists maintain that they are unable to resist the spirit of the place, in which they are so insignificant a minority. The House of Commons is made up of landlords, capitalists, and lawyers, who naturally attend to the interests of their own class. Nor can we be certain that a republican form of government is an advantage to the working classes; it is possible enough that in America a government controlled by the great capitalists and corporations of capitalists might be much more oppressive to the labourer than German imperialism. When we consider the growing power of the great business corporations headed by the energetic capitalists, of whom we hear so much, this fear is by no means chimerical. The social development of mankind has not yet reached its final stage, and may have many surprises in store for us. Republican institutions, controlled by millionaires on such a scale as is possible in America, would be a sight to astonish the world. The tendency towards such an unblest consummation is rapidly growing. Let the true friends of the American democracy be on their guard!

For the present, however, the militant socialism finds its bitterest and most formidable enemies in the older forms of government, in Germany and Russia. Of Russia it is unnecessary to speak. In Germany it was the aim of Lassalle to establish a working men's party, whose obvious policy would be one of alliance with the government against the capitalist class. Under the direction of Marx, who was a great hater of Prussia, the Social Democracy soon took up a position of strong hostility to the government; and Bismarck was long considered their special enemy. Even his state socialism they regarded as a very small concession to the claims of the workers, tending to strengthen a centralised government, which they detest. Some of his most famous measures in the direction of state socialism they entirely reprobated as devices for lending support to a military monarchy, to a high-handed bureaucracy and a hated police, in their struggle with the people.

It is not our intention here to offer a dogmatic opinion on these very debatable matters, but to indicate in a general way the relation of socialism to the state, especially as at present constituted. Obviously one of the gravest difficulties of our present political system is, how to secure an effective representation for the masses of the people. At present there is not even an approximation to it, nor is there likely to be for a considerable time to come. On this point the contention of socialists is, to a very large degree, well founded. Under present conditions the representation of the workmen in our parliaments is most inadequate, that is to say, representative government does not truly represent the mass of the people.

From these facts and considerations it will be obvious how misleading it is to identify socialism with state action. If we consider that the most convinced and pronounced socialists of the time have a confirmed distrust of the state, not only at present existing, but of almost any possible state, it must be at least misleading to say that socialism seeks to realise its reforms by the law or the state. Socialism is a form of economic organisation which may proceed from the state, but which may with not less hope of success proceed from the free initiative of the industrial people, and from local association. It is concerned with principles and tendencies which are more fundamental than government, at least as we understand it, with principles and tendencies involved in the ethical, social, and industrial life of the people. The action of the state may effect these, but it is their function much more to mould and control government. The economic policy of Bismarck was really a tribute to the great influences embodied in socialism. Both he and the Social Democrats have been only more or less wisely obeying the tendencies of their time. The strongest governments and the most resolute revolutionary parties are only phases of the massive and complex social movement of their time. They cannot essentially arrest or accelerate the tendencies of such a movement. Governments must obey them. Revolutionary parties must wait till the fulness of the time has come.

So much may be said with regard to the relation of socialism to the actual state. The questions we have been discussing depend largely on how far the state and its action conform to our ideal of what the state should be and do. It is the ideal of socialism that the state should be an association for the promotion of the true interests of all its members. But with this conception we rise to a higher and wider order of ideas.

CHAPTER VI

MORAL ASPECTS OF SOCIALISM

We have seen that socialism is a theory of social evolution based on a new principle of economic organisation, according to which industry should be carried on by co-operative workers jointly controlling the means of production. It is a principle which may be partially realised, even on the smallest scale. But its aim is vastly wider than to be a department merely in the existing economic order. It is a renovating principle, which seeks to leaven and transform the whole human society. First of all, it is an improved industrial condition, with co-operative labour as the normal or prevalent form; and on this as a basis it aims at establishing a higher and better state of society in all its members, departments, and interests. On the basis of a better economic order it aims at a more perfect realisation of the true, the beautiful, and the good, than has been attained in any previous era of mankind.

Socialism is a phase of social organisation following the development of capitalism and of the modern system of industry, and so transforming the latter as to make it more entirely serviceable to all mankind without distinction of class or sex, nation or creed, or colour. The subjection of labour and of women, the antagonism of classes, the conflicts of struggling nations and races—all of these, and every form of them it seeks to remove and abolish, and to realise the brotherhood of man. To the wars that fascinate and brutalise mankind, to narrow and degenerate patriotisms, to the military system which so oppresses the nations of the world, to class hatreds and jealousies, it is fundamentally opposed. The reader will see that the programme of social change implied in socialism is a wide and comprehensive one. The goal is far away and not easily to be attained. Obviously it is a transformation in human affairs, which, if ever it be fully realised, can be brought about only after long years, only after generations, it may be, of intelligent experiment and strenuous endeavour by the progressive part of mankind.

In the eyes of the cynical and faint-hearted, who habitually despair of human progress, such a theory will naturally seem ludicrous and Utopian. Even impartial and sympathetic judges, looking to the comparatively little advance made in the past, may doubt the practicability of such sanguine schemes of improvement. Principles having for their aim the abolition of war, and the realisation of the brotherhood of man, were they not announced in the Christian religion nearly nineteen hundred years ago? And yet we see the horizon of Christendom ever dark and lowering with the preparations for possible war. Hardly a year passes but the dark clouds grow black and menacing, and they too often break with devastating fury on some devoted portion of the earth. This is the response of Christian Europe after the new evangel has been for so many years proclaimed and nominally accepted. Who then will say that peace and brotherhood have any prospect of realisation ?

No one can deny that the process of realisation has been sadly incomplete, but we must emphatically assert that history gives no support to a gospel of pessimism. If we contrast our ideals with the realities of the present, we may well be shocked at the wretchedness of our failures ; but if we compare the practice of to-day with that of nineteen hundred years ago, the change for the better must be reckoned enormous. In those olden times inhuman cruelty and bloodshed were of familiar and everyday occurrence. Even the warfare of the present time is a display of courtesy, chivalry, and humanity, when compared with the barbarity of ancient days. Have those who disbelieve in human progress ever seen the instruments of torture that were in use in every European country not many generations ago ? These instruments of torture are now happily relegated to antiquarian museums. During the last fifty years alone, we have made a wonderful advance in humane feeling and action. If we continue to make a like advance during the next fifty, many of our most sanguine hopes will be realised. The despair of human progress entertained by so many has, to a large degree, its origin in their ignorance of the facts of history.

To say that the great principles of peace and brotherhood have never been realised is the mark of an external and mechanical way of looking at history. We believe that since they were first proclaimed they have been in continual process of realisation. Though their influence has been incomplete, it has been real, pervasive and powerful, leavening rough and wild forms of society, infusing into many a rugged and barbaric temperament an appreciation of what is humane, kindly and peaceful, and gradually establishing there a loyalty to the better forces, which, we hope, will one day govern the world. The history of the moral forces, too, is a process of development, which we can rightly measure only by a wide consideration of facts.

Still our progress, if we consider what it might be and ought to be, is deplorably slow. No one, therefore, who has an open mind and who has any real concern for human improvement, can exclude from consideration the possibility of devising better methods. As in the past, so in the present and future the course of thought and experience must have new views of society and fresh lessons of reform to disclose. In support of the moral forces and of all the educative and transforming influences which have done so much and are still doing so much for the good of the world, socialism proposes a new principle of economic organisation.

With many faults, the early teachers of socialism were men who had a large and generous faith in human progress. The pioneers of the world are usually such as do not despair of humanity, sanguine hearts in whom the tide of hope beats high. These are not the men who can accurately measure difficulties, or who can most scientifically analyse and determine the real and positive factors in social evolution; but they supply the motive power derivable from originality of conception, from fervid enthusiasm and from a perfect faith in human destiny and in the methods by which they propose to ameliorate it. The theories and procedure of such pioneers very frequently cannot bear criticism, but they have an abundant measure of that motive power in human improvement which criticism cannot supply.

But if early socialism was more remarkable for enthusiasm than sober-mindedness, the later teachers claim to be heard chiefly on critical and scientific grounds. Their purpose is not to advertise a new social panacea, but to trace the laws of social development, to show how the dominant real and positive tendencies of the time are working towards a new economic order. In human development the present has grown out of the past, and the future will grow out of the present only in accordance with laws of organic change, by a gradual course of adaptation, by continual trial and experiment on the part of intelligent men, who with their habits, laws, and institutions, must always be the prime factors in the great process of evolution. The task of scientific socialists is to point out that their ideal of progress is not a creature of the imagination, but irresistibly given in the prevailing tendencies of the social movement. In support therefore of the moral and other forces which already make for human improvement, socialism offers a new principle of economic organisation, not however as a Utopian scheme, but as a solid theory that will welcome the test both of criticism and experience. Unless it be given in the natural and necessary order of social development, socialism makes no claim to be considered. In point of fact, the greatest expounders of socialism insist too strongly on a necessary order of historical development, so strongly that they might almost be charged with fatalism. But however that may be, they advocate socialism on scientific grounds. They maintain that the strongest forces in the contemporary historic movement are on their side, that violence and agitation on the one hand, and repression on the other are merely the details and accessories of a vast organic movement, which they cannot essentially either accelerate or delay. Their function is first of all to tell us what is actually going on, to explain the principles, tendencies, and processes of a transformation which is already in action.

In comparison with the vast transformations determined by great forces operating over the civilised world, even what are usually called revolutions are of secondary importance. With or without the scenic display called the French Revolution, the ideas proclaimed therein would have been, more or less swiftly, more or less effectually realised. The time for them was fulfilled—the minds of men, not in one country, but in all countries embraced in the European system of states, were prepared for them. Revolutionary force and violence no more affect the course of history than rapids and falls modify the course of a river. With or without such interruptions, the river pursues the course determined by the physical structure of the country.

It will be obvious how these considerations must regulate and simplify the discussion of socialism. The question is not one of the schools or of party formulas; nor is it one to be settled by conspiracy, mere revolt or disturbance. It is a broad and general question of historic and social evolution.

Finality in human affairs is impossible, even if it were desirable. The new times raise fresh difficulties requiring new solutions, new arrangements, developed institutions. We have to consider whether socialism is the best and fittest form of economic organisation under the conditions which now prevail or tend to prevail. These conditions are of a most complex nature, technical and industrial, political and moral. Steam and electricity have revolutionised the technical and material basis of civilisation. We have now an educated, organised, and free democracy ; at least, one that is making continual progress in education, organisation, and freedom. The moral consciousness of men is becoming enlightened, humanised, and expanded ; it is alike more liberal, sympathetic, and exacting. Under such conditions, which are every day more fully developing themselves, can we expect that the old economic forms will suffice ? And if not, what are the new forms to be ?

In particular, let it not be forgotten that the dominant force in human history is the ethical one. Mechanical improvement is a most potent factor in social and economic development. Much will always depend on the material appliances, on the legal and political institutions, on the scientific discoveries and philosophical speculations of a given age or country ; but greater than any of these is the moral spirit that informs and governs the whole. How is it as regards the ethical spirit of socialism, not as it is found in this or that particular school, but as naturally associated with the fundamental principles of the theory ? On the moral side, how far is socialism likely to promote the good of man ?

Socialism may justly claim that it would mean a great advance in ethical development both in principle and practice. It is important first of all to point out what we may regard as the necessary minimum or indispensable basis of the socialistic conception of society. For the growth and progress of socialism it is essential that the workers attain to something like true insight into their position and prospects. They must see that they can succeed only by union, that the true interest of each is the interest of all; and to the capacity to see this they must add foresight, self-restraint, and moderation in acting upon it. Starting with the conception of a reasonable standard of living for all, it should be the enlightened self-interest of the vast majority to secure it by reasonable service to society and to be content with it. From this point of view we must therefore regard socialism as the combination or association of the workers to realise an enlightened conception of self-interest. Here individual interest and the common interest meet in harmony. It is on this foundation, which is both firm and broad, that socialism must build.

But the socialistic conception of ethics goes far beyond this. It is an ideal which is many-sided and far-reaching. If such an ideal could only be partially realised it would mark a wonderful advance in the history of mankind. Let us consider some of its aspects. Socialism involves a special condemnation of two great moral heresies, which are not only prevalent but practically triumphant in the present society. It is opposed, first, to the notion that over an immense area of action the commercial relation exhausts the range of human duty and responsibility. It has grown to be one of the commonest beliefs that economics and industry have laws of their own which are not regulated by moral principle; that business is controlled by laws of supply and demand, entitling us, for example, to buy the services of our fellow men at the cheapest rate, without regard to their health, character, or the consequences to society generally; that, competition being the rule in industry, we must take our own interest for our guide in its struggles and operations, though our action may result in ruin to our competitors. Such a theory is, of course, not always clearly formulated by those who practise it, but few will deny that it is a general principle of our competitive system. In direct opposition to all this, socialism maintains that industrial operations should be made subservient to human good; and that the moral law should control the relations of business and the whole field of human action every day of the week.

It is not less opposed to another and kindred heresy, which is almost equally prevalent, that a human being may be degraded into an instrument or commodity. This position of degradation is precisely the lot of the majority of men and women in the present industrial order. In the labour market the workman seeks to sell his labour-force, and if he is lucky enough to find a purchaser he has his price; if not, he and his family enjoy the supreme privilege of freedom, they may starve. But assuming that he is fortunate enough to find a price, we must recognise that in most civilised countries he has to work under conditions as to wages and length of hours, &c., that leave him neither strength, leisure, nor opportunity to develop the qualities of a man and a citizen. In the vast industrial processes of production and exchange he is but an item, a small part of a great mechanism. Herein is the office and function of the working man, to serve as an intelligent labouring machine; and in this function his force and capacity are for the most part exhausted. Anything worthy of the name of culture, true intellectual and artistic enjoyment of life and of nature, an intelligent appreciation of his duties and position—these are for him impossible, or possible only on the most meagre scale. Evidently the first condition of improvement is the general reduction of the hours of work to eight per day. When the hours of labour are generally reduced to eight, the worker may be a man and a citizen. At present he is just rising to a consciousness of his wrongs, the first step, we hope, towards his deliverance and real participation in the world's heritage of culture and in the rights of manhood and citizenship.

On this eight hours' platform, then, reformers of every class and party may be invited to unite. Many of the critics of the democracy complain that the masses are not sufficiently educated and intelligent for their new responsibilities. Let them prove their sincerity by joining in a universal movement for an eight hours' working day. In this country there has been a very real progress through the general reduction of the working day to nine hours; but in many industries we have not reached that point, and in some of our newest, as railways and tramways, it is still deplorably long. On the Continent and in America long hours are too prevalent.

In this matter the conditions of labour for working men are bad enough, but for working women they are decidedly worse. In all our large towns there are thousands of women trying to live on low and precarious wages, gained by labour which is continued for mercilessly long hours and most trying to the physique; and, at the most susceptible time of life, they are exposed to constant solicitation, especially from the members of the richer classes. Poorly fed, demoralised by long hours in rooms that are often overcrowded and insanitary, with a glittering and seductive alternative continually presented to them as a way of escape from a life of hardship, can we wonder that so many of the daughters of the poor are induced to part with virtue and health and the hope of a good and honourable life? If the conditions of their life are such that they are continually solicited, tempted, or driven to the mercenary degradation and debasement of what should be best and highest in human nature, the primary responsibility must rest with our social system and its upholders, and not with the wretched victims. Surely it is a fitting result of a commercial and competitive system that even love has thus become mercenary and saleable, has been made common, vile, and brutish. If systems as well as men are to be known by their fruits, we cannot remain in any further doubt as to the merits of the existing order of things.

Against all these heresies, socialism must raise an absolute protest; against mercenary love in all its forms, against the degradation of humanity through bad economic conditions, and against the extrusion of morality from the industrial life of men in the name of any theory whatsoever.

On these points, while socialism has nothing novel

to suggest, it certainly presents morality in a new light, and with regard to the more positive aspects of ethical theory, it gives fresh illustration to the highest and best teaching of the world. Under a socialistic system the great field of ambition and the chief scope for high and useful activity will be found in the service of society. It recognises that the ideal of human conduct is the service of man; but it sees not less clearly that as man can be realised only in society, and as individual character and happiness can be duly developed only under fitting and favourable economic and social conditions, it is to the service of society in its various forms that we are specially called to devote ourselves. Service rendered to the human society, beginning with the family, and expanding through the wider social groups and the nation, till it embraces the whole human race: such is the moral law of socialism. But it is given to few to render service on the large scale. The duties of the majority of men are circumscribed by their limited capacity, and by the fixed conditions of their social and geographical position. In the language of the Parable of the Good Samaritan, our service must be given to our neighbour; and our neighbours in the prescribed circle of human relations are those of our own household, those of the same street and village, those whom we meet in the daily routine, as defined by nature and the actual circumstances and facts of life. But in the narrowest sphere the opportunities of usefulness, well-doing, and even of heroism are not few, and happily the better souls that rise to the level of such occasions are more in number than is often supposed. And to such as have proved their worth in the humblest lot, an ever-widening sphere of good and noble activity is continually open, so that the heroism which has endured and worked in simple unconsciousness of itself may become a far-shining example of well-doing over the wide world and to the latest generations of mankind.

An enlightened and well-regulated self-interest, the family affections, civic feeling and a healthy and legitimate patriotism all find their due place in a socialistic conception of life. The relations of men to each other will more and more take the form of a free interchange of services, and in this they will find their inspiration, but they will be graded according to their significance for the service of mankind.

Thus in the service of society there is a place and a value assigned to the narrowest as well as to the widest forms of useful activity, from the little sphere of the mother quietly tending her children in the humblest cottage to the far-reaching activity of the greatest pioneers in scientific and industrial progress, like Newton and James Watt, whose discoveries and inventions have beneficially influenced the entire human race. And corresponding to the variety in the extent of service is the diversity of its intensity, rising from the honest and simple performance of the ordinary duties of life to the highest phases of heroism and self-sacrifice.

We are not to suppose that such an ideal is likely to become the working conception of duty among average men for a long time to come; but it is already the accepted rule of the generous *élite*, and through them, we hope, will influence the mass. Further, as in the arrangements of socialism social service is offered as the chief field of ambition, it will tend most effectively to make the self-interest of the aspirant coincide with the good of society. In this way the co-operative ideal could be made an instrument of human progress to a degree that men who are accustomed only to the half-false and conventional moral standards of the time cannot conceive.

How much of the moral energy, devotion, and enthusiasm of the past has been wasted on false and pernicious ideals, in useless penance, maceration, and self-immolation, in bigotry, superstition, and pedantry, in blind and passionate patriotisms, in selfish jealousies, and personal vanities? Simeon Stylites standing on his pillar and for thirty years wasting his body and driving himself to madness by exposure and maceration is only a supreme instance of mistaken and unavailing devotion to a wrong conception of duty. There are many amongst us still who toil and suffer with a zeal and futility similar to that of Simeon, and who should be invited to come down from their pillar and help the crowd below in their actual struggles and sorrows. That it may be wise and effective, social service should be guided by science and the best available light.

Such an ideal of service is by no means new. As we have said before, it is the highest accepted morality, and was enjoined on His followers by the Founder of Christianity in the most sacred way—'But I am in the midst of you as he that serveth,' 'Whosoever would be first among you, shall be servant of all,' 'Inasmuch as ye did it unto one of the least of these My brethren, ye did it unto Me.' Service rising up to self-sacrifice for the good of men is the ideal of the Christian life, which through centuries of Christian history has been more or less loyally cherished by the purest and devoutest hearts; but it has too frequently been a dead letter. According to this principle the greatest is only the chief servant of the Christian society, and imperial hands even yet in imitation of the Master wash the feet of beggars. Pity that the history of a principle so noble should have proved to so great a degree a record of failure and travesty!

Socialism may well accept it as its ethical corner-stone. The greatest and highest man in society is he who renders the best and noblest service. In the words of Louis Blanc, 'The day will come when it will be recognised that each one's debt to his fellow-men is in proportion to the strength and intelligence he has received from God; and it will be a part worthy of genius to assert its legitimate empire, not by the amount of the tribute it will levy on society, but by the greatness of the services that it will render to it.' The realisation of such an ideal may be far off, but it is worth striving for; and if the world is indeed a place of hope and progress and continual development in all that is good and beautiful, it cannot for ever be delayed.

Thus we see that socialism most powerfully makes appeal to the entire ascending scale of human motives, from an enlightened self-interest to the highest self-sacrifice. But its special function is to provide for their effectual operation forms of economic and social organisation that are not only real but open up widening vistas of growth and expansion.

So much for the purely ethical side of the question. A further point on which we must particularly insist is that a system of associated workers jointly owning the means of production and wielding the best machinery in the service of man is both ethically and scientifically on a higher plane than the present system of precarious and degraded labour as employed by competing capitalists. Such a method of free co-operative labour applied to agriculture, for example, would certainly be a great improvement on the present English land system. Only through combination and co-operation can the cultivators procure and work the best machinery. Only by combination can they hold their own against powerful individuals, and especially against the middleman and usurer, who have so long and so often been the enemies of the peasant farmer. With the best machinery and co-operative labour, the cultivators could introduce the most scientific methods of farming, could have leisure and opportunity for culture and health. If such a system could be generally adopted it would change the face of the world. In every country where it has been introduced it has already proved to be a beneficent agency. Men should therefore work for its diffusion and expansion in obedience to ideals that grow wider and more beautiful. And thus it would ever more become a system of free industry, calling forth and exercising high qualities of intelligent co-operation, regard for others, regard for method and order, forethought, and all the elements of the social discipline required for the effectual application of capital and of the highest science to the service of the workers. The same method could be applied to mines and factories with similar results, both industrial and moral. For the success of such a system it would be essential that the ethical advance of men should keep pace with the industrial improvement. It would be a marvellous ethical and social ideal if it could be attained!

If it could be attained! It will no doubt be urged that theoretical considerations as to what is ideally best are all very well in their way, but that the affairs of the world are controlled by practical forces; that life is based on real and fixed conditions, which impose an invincible barrier to vague aspiration; that there are in fact insuperable objections to the realisation of socialism in the constitution of human nature itself.

CHAPTER VII

DIFFICULTIES AND OBJECTIONS

THE difficulties in the way of the socialistic ideal may be summed up as follows:

It is too lofty a theory for human nature. The only motive power in human nature that is sufficiently solid and durable to bear the wear and tear of practice is individual self-interest. Upon each man must rest the responsibility of shaping his own career. This is not a perfect method, but in a general way it is the only working one. Moreover, in every form of society, whatever the safeguards that may be devised, the able, energetic, persevering, ambitious, and not seldom the unscrupulous, will assert themselves and occupy the first place. If the present system were abolished to-morrow, it would merely be a change of masters.

The co-operative system of society does not provide an adequate check against vice and improvidence of every kind. Under the present system, when each man has to act on his own responsibility, nature provides a sure and effective remedy against error. The penalty is failure, ruin it may be. Improvidence, thoughtlessness, drunkenness, even incapacity meet severe retribution. The method is often a cruel one, but it is a patent and well-established law of human progress against which protest is useless; and it has the undeniable result that the fittest prevail and survive. It is not an ideal system; but the work of the world is carried on under it, whereas socialism might result in a deadlock.

The industrial arrangements of modern civilisation are too complex to be so controlled by any administrative authority. England especially, with her enormously large and complicated business, is one of the last countries where a thoroughgoing socialism proceeding from the central government would be likely to succeed, notwithstanding the exceptionally well-developed public spirit of her citizens.

A socialistic state would afford too great scope for despotism and the spirit of routine. Repressing individual initiative and enterprise, and affording unbounded temptation and opportunity to an intolerable officialism, it would menace civilisation with the domination of pedants, bureaucrats, and policemen. Such a system, swarming with officials, high and low, would be worthy only of China. If it were established, it would be one of the first duties of a progressive society to shake it off. It is the supreme interest of free men to resist official tyranny, wherever it exists, and to establish conditions of unrestricted progress. Under a state socialism, however, the old despotism would be renewed in a worse form than ever, inasmuch as on the theory of socialism the people's means of subsistence would be under the control of the official class.

These objections may be more comprehensively stated thus:

1. It is impracticable, because inconsistent with the known and tried principles of human nature;

with that permanent groundwork of human nature which is independent of historic evolution, on which, indeed, evolution itself depends.

2. It is impossible, because no central authority could control interests so numerous, so enormous and complicated.

3. Even if practicable, it is not the way to promote the social ideal of a free and happy development, because tending to interfere with individual liberty.

Now, if it were proposed to introduce a system of socialism ready-made and without a testing course of experiment, of preparation and co-operation with the natural tendencies of social improvement, these objections would be insuperable. Such a thing, however, could not be reasonably contemplated. Scarcely any theorist would be bold enough to propose that society should forthwith repudiate its present methods and adopt a new and untried system of social organisation. It is, indeed, a common fault of socialistic theorists that they begin at the wrong end and indicate as the starting-point what even on their own principles is really the goal of a long process of social development, laying down as if for immediate realisation a programme which it would require generations to carry out. But all systems have a right to be tried by their fundamental principles, and not by the one-sided utterances of particular exponents. We have often had reason to protest against such a conception of socialism, and we must again repeat that socialism is not like a new style of coat, which is intended to be put on and off at pleasure. It is a new principle of social organisation, which, if it prevail at all, must be wrought into the very framework of the living society. Experience alone can really prove whether it can become a working conception of society.

As we have said before, the great changes of history are not brought in ready-made and complete. They come in by gradual steps, by insensible degrees. At first we see here and there a few streaks of dawn indicating the approach of a brighter era, and it may be long before the light gathers in a large and massive volume sufficient to overspread the world. In this connection we should do well to consider the labour and time it cost to set up the present system of constitutional freedom, which, if not a perfect system, is at least a vast improvement on the era that preceded it. It is a political form which was shaped in the course of centuries by men who saw the needs of their time and had the capacity to satisfy them ; it was found to work well, and is now the accepted theory of the countries that are politically most advanced. It was gradually evolved out of previously existing facts through discussion and experiment, failure and struggle. Things move much more rapidly now, but if society is to rise out of its present condition of unsettlement to a new unity and harmony of interests, the transition must be made in a similar way.

Yet even with our present experience, and in view of the prevailing facts of social evolution, it is possible to overrate the force of the above objections against socialism. Some of them, indeed, spring from an entire misunderstanding of the subject. We have already protested against the identification of socialism with state action. If socialism carried with it a system of pedantic and intermeddling officialism, if it meant that a central authority should press with its superincumbent weight on the free play of local and individual life, it would not be worth discussing for a moment. An energetic central government would be required in any well-ordered society, but the effectiveness of such a government could be secured and maintained only by a wide devolution of functions and by a wise restriction of its action to certain necessary duties. It may be that under a socialistic system the central government would need greatly to extend its control over such large industrial factors as railways, but the first and most essential condition of success would lie in the development of local energy.

Having made those explanations, we shall now proceed to discuss the objections that may be urged against the possibility of a society based on co-operative industry.

First objection: socialism impracticable because inconsistent with human nature. It is obvious that there is in human nature a permanent groundwork which all social reformers must take into account. It is possible, however, greatly to overrate the strength and extent of this, as has certainly been done by many economists and moralists deficient in philosophic training and in the historic faculty. Human nature is not the fixed quantity that many believe it to be, but varies almost indefinitely in accordance with the laws of social evolution, and adapts itself with marvellous plasticity to new conditions. Human nature at Athens under Pericles is hardly recognisable as the same thing with human nature of the Australian aborigines. Man in Europe has been a very different being from man in China. How far is the energetic and enterprising New Englander the same as the inert native of Bengal or the member of a Russian commune with his fixed and conservative routine of life? The groundwork is indeed the same, but the possibilities of variation and development in human character are very great; and in institutions the range and variety is wonderful, from the unorganised condition of a tribe of Bushmen to the government of the British Empire. And yet even the latter is imperfect and inadequate to the wants of a more exacting time. How different, again, is the government of Britain from that of Germany! In short, very few of us realise that capacity of variation and adaptation in human nature which has so powerfully contributed to give us the dominion of the world.

Still, we must admit the strength and solidity of self-interest as a permanent factor in human nature. For reasons which it would here be tedious and unnecessary to explain, this is a fact which cannot be otherwise. Self-interest is a constant factor with action that may be calculated, and is part and parcel of human nature itself.

With this principle in its reasonable and legitimate applications, however, socialism has no quarrel whatsoever. It claims better than any other economic system to satisfy the right and healthy interests, needs, and aspirations of men, not of a narrow minority of men, but of all men. Whilst under the present system the interests, physical, intellectual, and spiritual, of the majority are sacrificed to the excessive and unnatural claims of a small minority, socialism aims at a more equitable distribution both of duty and of the opportunities of enjoyment and individual development. The ideal of a well-constituted society is one which, while affording free play to individual energy and initiative, makes them subservient to the general good. It is the aim of socialism to accomplish this, only by recognising, however, that it is the whole body of individuals whose interests should be thus promoted, and not an exceptionally favoured minority. The quarrel of socialism is with the excessive and abnormal development of private and individual interests. It is the excess of individualism that all societies must dread. How often have we to complain of the excessive development of the public and social spirit? What has led to violent revolutions and the ruin of states? Has it not usually been the development of private and class interests to a degree utterly inconsistent with the public weal? What ruined ancient Rome? What was the cause of the French Revolution? To anyone who has an elementary acquaintance with history such questions are superfluous.

Self-interest can be trusted as a principle of human nature only when placed under higher ethical guidance. This is a truth continually overlooked by orthodox economists and by all classes of men living under the present competitive system. Nothing, indeed, is so amazing as the honour that has been accorded to this principle of self-interest. In a civilisation calling itself Christian it is the acknowledged motive power in our economics; it is the law of business; it is supposed to be the great instrument of progress; and under various euphemisms it has been preached in season and out of season to the young as a rule of life and a guiding principle of a worthy ambition—in sublime unconsciousness that all this is in absolute contradiction to the religious principles which we profess. The struggle to get on, the intense individualism which has been generally accepted, in practice at least, as the chief end of man cannot be reconciled with any religious theory of life. Even in most heathen communities the theory of every man for himself would be repudiated as destructive of the natural charities of life and subversive of the necessary order of society. We are told, by men intimately acquainted with India, that a beggar could travel from one end of the country to another, and that he would everywhere find the natives ready to give him a share of what they have. The adherents of economic orthodoxy should consider whether their theory does not really tend to anarchy and the dissolution of society in its primary elements. Self-interest will always have a large and permanent place in the evolution of humanity, but it must be subordinated to higher principles of moral and social order. The intensely individualised forms of it which now prevail are, we trust, a passing phase in the history of mankind. In the past they have not been a normal characteristic of men, and will in the future, we hope, give place to a milder and more social state of feeling.

While it is true that the struggle of individual interest has in the past been an instrument of progress, we should in this matter avoid exaggeration. The struggle of interests in the past has much more generally been one of societies of men against each other. It has been a struggle of men organised in society, and the victory has been very greatly due to improvements in organisation, to the higher ethical and social virtue, which has been as the cement that bound the citizens together, and made them strong and immovable in the shock of conflict. In general, too, the best and most capable individuals are born and thrive only in healthy and well-balanced societies. It is an extremely narrow view to regard the struggle of individual interests as the exclusive or even as the chief instrument of progress. The progress of mankind has consisted and must consist chiefly and fundamentally in the growth of the social virtues, and in the development of better methods and appliances of social organisation.

The advocates of the prevalent individualism have not been remarkable for their knowledge of history, but they ought to remember that their system is but of yesterday, and that the general rule, justified by the experience of mankind, has been social control of private and individual interests. Such social control has, indeed, been a necessity of existence. The great problem of the future is to harmonise the newly won idea of freedom with social unity and security.

Nor can one see that there will not be sufficient room for the play of a just and honourable ambition in a socialistic state. As teacher and man of science, as organiser and director of industry, or as statesman, the most energetic and highly gifted youth would find in the public service an adequate scope for his talents and a competent reward from an appreciative society. Such large scope for ambition as a Gladstone or a Salisbury found in the service of society will assuredly be sufficient for any reasonable man. Even now the most honourable and the most coveted positions are to be found in the social sphere.

Still, we need not doubt that in the best-arranged society the exaggerated and degenerate forms of self-interest will for a long time be very strong. Individual self-help has been for so many generations inculcated as a motive to success, especially in the Anglo-Saxon world, that we cannot expect without great difficulty to establish better habits and a better social feeling. On the other hand, ignorance, improvidence, mutual suspicion, and the helplessness intensified and prolonged by the hereditary disabilities of centuries have so incapacitated and demoralised the mass of the workers in most countries that a reasonable and effective union in pursuit of a common interest cannot for many years be expected. For the removal of those evils and for the establishment of a higher order of things we must depend on the growing intelligence of the body of the people, and on the wise co-operation of all classes. Why should it be impossible so to enlighten and moralise all classes that the best way for the whole may be found in a reasonable solidarity of interests; and the best endowed may seek their chief good, not in materialistic rewards, but in honourable social distinction, and in the consciousness of having served their fellow-men well and worthily? Such a high ideal cannot be soon or easily realised, but it may at least be possible to minimise individual excess, and so to curb the anti-social extravagance now prevailing that the best schemes of human progress may not be rendered futile by egotism, improvidence, and folly.

At this point we may notice Cairnes' objection[1]

[1] See *Some Leading Principles of Political Economy newly expounded*, p. 323.

to socialism based on the allegation that our industry cannot be carried on without a large accumulated capital; that in the present system private self-interest is a sufficient motive for accumulation, but that under socialism no sufficient motive could be found. To this it may simply be replied that innumerable societies and many municipalities have already a large accumulated capital, which no one proposes to squander. Against corruption we have a safeguard in publicity. Incapacity and mismanagement are checked by continual criticism. For a co-operative system of industry, as for a democratic system of government, publicity and the watchful criticism rendered possible by publicity are essential. The mass of men are really not so unable to comprehend their common interests as is implied in this objection. If the co-operative system of industry were otherwise found to work best, we can see in this point no valid reason against it.

There remains another point on which human improvidence as a factor in social evolution might have a fatal result in a socialistic society. This refers to the population question. In a socialistic arrangement of society it is alleged that parental responsibility would be so relaxed, there would be such an increase in the number of children, and in population, that it would soon outstrip the means of subsistence available in any country, and eventually on the planet itself. Most socialists entirely disregard this objection; and it must be said that if society were wisely organised, if wealth and its natural sources were distributed with a rational regard to population, and if our industry were reasonably scientific, the question of population is one that affects only the remote future. We must educate and train the people in rational habits, in free self-control, in the knowledge of natural laws, and in the recognition of our mutual duties and responsibilities; we must, above all, correct and improve our social and economic system. A nation with its soil half cultivated, with an empire consisting so largely of sparsely peopled colonies, has no right to appeal to the law of population as an excuse for its shortcomings. Such a plea is really a confession of its impotence to overcome the most elementary difficulties in social organisation. We are therefore justified in maintaining that the pressing question is one of social reform at home and of emigration.

At the same time the problem is one not of possibilities, but of practicabilities. There has always been relative over-population; that is, there has been an excess of population in particular countries and at particular times as compared with the available means of subsistence. We may sooner or later find that the increase of population may make the question a very practical one. How far the practice of limiting families, which has become so prevalent, may solve the problem we cannot say. While it is a practice open to very grave objections, we must recognise its influence.

If ever it be realised on a large scale, socialism would have to meet the difficulties inherent in the problem. While we cannot see that it has any easy and conclusive solution to offer, we cannot admit that it is in any essential respect worse placed than the present system. Under a co-operative system of industry, each man would have to do his share of social service, and would be mainly responsible for the bringing up of his children. It is to be hoped that the mass of men would be so advanced as at once to meet these obligations. For the residuum, who might decline, some form of compulsion would be necessary. The fundamental law, 'If any will not work neither shall he eat,' would need to be applied to them. For hopelessly improvident parents the penalty might be separation and compulsory work. The strength of socialism would be found in the fact that laziness, improvidence, and waste would be discouraged by the general consensus of feeling and opinion; that the whole community would be interested in cultivating forethought and self-control; disregard for such virtues would be a sin against the whole of society. Organised in local groups, or according to their respective trades, the average workman would have a sure grasp of his economic and industrial position, and he would, as in the mediæval guilds, be able once more to live under tolerably clear and fixed conditions. The uncertainty and haphazard of the present are assuredly not conducive to habits of forethought and reasonable self-control.

If it really be the tendency of socialism seriously to undermine individual responsibility in these and other matters, we must at once admit that it has no case. But we cannot see that the difficulty applies to any rational theory of co-operative industry.

At any rate, no reasonable man will expect an absolute solution of a question that has perplexed statesmen in every age. All that can reasonably be demanded of socialism is, that it supply a better working solution than the present. And what is our present method? In all countries of Christendom what multitudes of children are born to privation, neglect, disease, vice, and premature death! In ancient times it was the practice, as it still is in China, to expose children to perish in the open air, that the parents might be relieved of the burden of bringing them up—the recognised method of limiting population. We are not so frank and rigorous in our cruelty. The ranks of our children are thinned by the more gradual operation of hunger, neglect, and disease. In some of our large towns, out of a thousand children that are born, more than two hundred die in the first year. Under the present system each head of a family bears the responsibility for his own children; but how does he fulfil it? Is this condition of things a solution of a great social question? Do any of us fully realise the cruelty and barbarity of the child-exposure of the present time in Christian countries? Nor is this the worst. Of those who escape early death, how many survive with weakened constitution, and when they grow up, how many are exposed to a life of degradation and infamy!

We pride ourselves on the abolition of the old heathen customs; is our own practice so much better? Under any social system it may be long before the ethical and social status of men is so raised as to place the matter on a tolerable footing, but in controverting socialism do not let us imagine that we have solved a great question, when we have merely shut our eyes to our own failures.

Second objection: socialism impossible because no central authority could control interests so enormous as are involved in the industrial life of modern society.

With reference to this objection it must be admitted that it is the inevitable tendency of civilisation, especially since the great technical changes due to steam and electricity, to become more delicate, complex, and gigantic. The extent and variety of national interests increase enormously. Would it not overtax the strength and capacity of any central power to control arrangements so vast and elaborate?

It may at once be admitted that the government of England as at present organised could not be expected greatly to extend its control over the central arrangements of industry. Though the post and telegraph are well managed under state ownership and control, it would, under present circumstances, for obvious reasons, probably be hazardous to nationalise the railway system. The chief reason is that the government cannot overtake its present work. But as regards the general question it should be pointed out—

(1) That the same technical causes which have produced our vast and elaborate social mechanism also tend to simplicity and efficiency. The mightiest steamship obeys a small helm. An army of a million men is moved by a telegraph message.

(2) The objection in itself does not apply to countries with a comparatively simple range of interests, like Denmark and Switzerland. Compared with this country, even the United States presents a moderately easy problem. Its interests are home interests; it is a self-contained and self-supporting country. With its enormous range of economic and political affairs, involving it with almost every country of the world, England is in quite an abnormal position.

(3) It is to be hoped that the government of the future will be less identified with the adjusting of party mechanism, the artificial life of courts and of the higher society, with the intrigues of place-hunters and of diplomacy, with war and conquest, and foreign administration ; and that it will give its chief attention to the directing of the industrial life, on which the welfare of a people really depends. The democracy will insist that the good of the people is not promoted by a form of government that gives such a disproportionate place to family and class interests and to intermeddling with foreign nations all over the habitable globe. In this respect social progress has to aim, not so much at an extension as a rearrangement of central control. Government should be directed from obsolete or class interests to the real and living public interests.

(4) There must be an adequate development of local government, giving to the people the management of their own affairs in the parish, municipality, etc. In England the movement is only beginning, and its possibilities are practically unlimited. The effect of our aristocratic government in the past has been to crush local energy and initiative, and to repress the free life of the people. We have at last begun to understand that in countries less advanced than ourselves local institutions have been much better preserved and fostered than with us. It is only the crassest ignorance or wilful misrepresentation on the part of the opponents of socialism to object to it as throwing the burden of social work on the central government. Socialism demands the fullest development of local energy, the free organisation of

the people in such forms as are required by the exigencies of modern life, such organisation not to be dictated by a central body, but to proceed out of the spontaneous and natural movement of the people through an intelligent appreciation of their needs.

(5) It is hardly fair to draw any inference unfavourable to socialism from the comparative inefficiency of our present Civil Service and higher officials. Our higher education has been preposterous, and antiquated to a degree absolutely amazing in a people that calls itself practical. Greek and Latin verse, ancient mythology, and other antiquated and almost useless forms of knowledge and intellectual acrobatism, have occupied an altogether unjustifiable amount of attention. Our governors, it should be added, are drawn almost entirely from a small percentage of the population, from the upper classes. If education were rendered thoroughly modern and efficient, if talent were trained and welcomed wherever found, and applied to the most honourable of all service, the service of society, we should have a body of public officers such as the world has not yet seen.

(6) At the very least the country would possess the same amount of brains and business capacity as before. Only, instead of each capitalist managing his business at his own risk, we should have the best talent of the country conducting it in the service of society; and whereas at present there is neither unity nor common method, industrial operations would be systematically and organically carried on.

Third objection: socialism inconsistent with freedom. It is very generally assumed that socialism would involve a great curtailment of individual freedom.

It is not easy to understand how such an idea has arisen, unless it be that men still associate socialism with the life in barracks supposed to be contemplated by theorists like Fourier and Owen, and which was believed to necessitate a minute and vexatious interference with human liberty on subjects that least admit of regulation. But however the idea may have arisen, whether it be based like most of the prevailing opinions regarding socialism on mere ignorance and misrepresentation, there can be no doubt that it is widespread and deep-rooted.

Now, nothing can be more certain than that under the present system the freedom of the mass of men is merely nominal. If attained at all, it can be attained only at the expense of security, at the risk of sacrificing the means of subsistence; it is a choice of working under the prescribed conditions, which are frequently unhealthy, degrading and dangerous, or of starving. Not seldom there is no choice at all, but compulsory starvation and the wretchedness of pauperism. Of course there is the alternative of emigration, but for great numbers, especially of those advanced in years, that too is excluded; and in many colonies the labour market is overstocked. Even in America great numbers have at times been unable to find work. Such freedom is a mockery and delusion. There can be no substantial or desirable freedom that is not based on economic security, on the possession of a home, and on well-established means of subsistence and of cultivation both of body and mind.

Our present system of industrial relations is in theory regulated by free contract. In a country where land and capital are virtually the monopoly of a class, there must be a vast multitude of contracts that are only nominally free. When land is required for building or industrial purposes, the landholder can exact his own terms; the contract is not free. Did the Irish peasant and the landlord negotiate on equal terms? Does the London man of business meet the owner of his premises on an equal footing? He has to deal with a powerful monopolist for that which is to him essential and indispensable. Scarcely anywhere or at any time, even with the unrestricted right of combination, does the workman meet the capitalist on equal terms.

The strength of this objection against socialism, indeed, consists chiefly in three gigantic fallacies:

(1) In the free competition so much belauded by the opponents of socialism it is constantly assumed that the contest is waged on equal terms. As we have seen, such an assumption is intolerable. The truth is almost precisely the reverse. For men who have neither land nor capital the contest must be most disadvantageous.

(2) It is very generally assumed that the contest is for success, for the prizes of life. Such an idea can be entertained only by those who never look below the surface of society. The present competitive system is one that exposes to hazard the daily bread, the health and character of millions. For thousands of barmaids and sempstresses entering on such a competition in our large towns death would be infinitely preferable.

(3) In the one-sided 'individualism' that is so much preached under the name of self-help, there is in fact a perpetual confusion of two totally different

things, individual struggle and individual success. In the individual struggle hundreds of thousands are utterly sacrificed. Real and substantial success is attained only by the few at the expense of the many, who are reduced to economic subjection. Individualism really means the struggle of all and the success of a few. For the immense majority it means the loss of real manhood, and of much that constitutes the glory and beauty of human personality. For most men it implies the obscuration and diminution, and even utter obliteration, of all that is good and noble in individuality. And even for those who do succeed to their heart's desire in the often ignoble contest for wealth, what real good ensues? After all, a man, however huge his capacity, can eat and drink only to a limited extent. A competent portion of the good things of this life can be obtained with very moderate means, and beyond that a Rothschild or a Rockefeller can obtain no more real enjoyment. The rest is vanity, labour and sorrow, cupidity and rapacity. The accumulation of enormous fortunes for private and selfish ends is an enormity and a monstrosity, tending to the growth of parasitism, luxury, extravagance and vice, to the demoralisation of society, to civil disturbance, and to the ruin of states. In such a conflict of egotisms both the successful and the unsuccessful suffer. The temperate, well-balanced, and healthy development of individual character can no longer be maintained. Carried to its final issues such an individual struggle can end only in social ruin.

It should also be pointed out that the 'individual' as understood in the existing society is the male head of the house. It is even yet a kind of half-conscious assumption with many that the wife and children are his property, and though the cruder forms of such a theory have mostly disappeared, it still largely colours our conceptions, to the extent that, in view of the disproportionate claims and rights of the male head, those of wife and children are very greatly sacrificed.

Under a co-operative system there would, of course, be an effective organisation of industry, but the workers would understand that such organisation must tend to the good of all, and it would not be felt as a burden. It would be a free and intelligent organisation, in which compulsion and restraint could be reduced to a minimum. In comparison with most work as at present carried on it would be a pleasure. When we consider the waste of human labour arising from strikes, commercial crises, from the idleness of the rich, and of the vagabond and demoralised poor; when we consider the imperfections of our system of distribution, and the incomplete development of machinery, we can easily understand that the hours of toil could be greatly reduced, and yet the work of the world be ever so much better done. At present the workman too frequently goes about his task as an unwilling and servile drudgery, without interest in its excellence and speedy completion; from such labour we can make no inference as to what true artistic and thorough work might be under right conditions.

Under a socialistic state it would be a natural and universal duty for all men to render some useful service to society. Only those who were disabled by sickness, accident, or old age would be relieved from an obvious obligation. But as the hours of labour would be greatly reduced, there would, after the necessary work of social industry was over, remain ample leisure for all men for the cultivation and enjoyment of all that is good, wholesome and beautiful. Each one could follow his natural bent and develop his native aptitudes in mechanical invention, in gardening and the culture of flowers, in athletics, music or painting, in science and literature.

Under these circumstances there would be a rich and varied development of natural capacity in both sexes, such as we cannot even at present conceive. At present how many a fair and noble endowment is suffered to go to waste in country villages and in the streets of our large towns! How many a finely constituted temperament utterly wasted and done to death under the hard and cruel pressure of uncongenial and adverse conditions! How many a Raphael and Beethoven, how many a poet and statesman have passed away in village and street without rendering any worthy service to mankind! Here, indeed, is a new field of development for the human race.

Through the development of mechanical invention to ever greater degrees of power and efficiency, and especially through the perfecting of our social organisation, the labour and skill of each would more and more be made directly subservient to the good of all. Man's victory over nature, and over the unregenerate residuum within himself, would be rendered more and more complete. It would be a real dominion of the world, a true ethical freedom.

CHAPTER VIII

PROSPECTS OF SOCIALISM

WE have in the last chapter reviewed some of the leading difficulties and objections that stand in the way of the general realisation of a co-operative form of industry. It will be seen that we have been dealing with an economic theory which has been only partially realised, with a theory of industrial organisation towards which, even in the opinion of its adherents, only the tendencies are growing and the conditions preparing. Much of the discussion, therefore, is merely conjectural and speculative. While inquiry may and does prepare the way for action, theories of social progress can be duly tested by experience alone.

We believe that the co-operative form of industry encourages the brightest hopes of social improvement; but when we consider the fatal prevalence of egotism, improvidence, and folly in human nature and in human history, doubt as to the general realisation of the system is only too legitimate. Without a great moral advance socialism may be regarded as impracticable. Without a great increase of enlightened self-control, and of regard for our fellow-men, a true freedom cannot be generally realised. Freedom must be associated with willing loyalty to law, especially moral law. It must be wedded to law and order, to truth and knowledge. The growth of free self-control and of an enlightened regard for the common good is indispensable to the development of socialism.

Thus, according to the point of view, and in proportion to the hopefulness of the inquirer, it may be regarded as the strength or weakness of socialism that it implies such a great moral advance in the development of mankind. Moral improvement is what all good men desire for themselves and others. Socialism proposes a method of industry fitted to serve both as a basis and as a framework for such moral improvement. Is it to be condemned because it is too exacting? Or is it to be commended because it supplies the economic conditions for a better moral order? Whether the theory be too high for human nature the future alone can decide. Let us hope that it is not. Let us also remember that, in any case, its realisation cannot be accomplished in a day, and that it must first take root among the most advanced of our industrial population if it is to succeed at all. Moreover, the ethical progress of men must go hand in hand with the industrial and political; progress must be mutual and solid; advance in one department of social life presupposes and necessitates advance in every other.

But it is the main contention of socialists that their theory of economic progress does not depend for its realisation on hopes more or less tainted with Utopianism. They are aware also that the evolution of society does not turn merely on the results of theoretical controversy and discussion. It is determined by the general tendency of the strongest forces. If socialism come at all, it must come as the consummation of the dominant forces of the existing society. The wishes and likings of men, the schemes of theorists, the arguments of debaters and controversialists, the efforts of agitators and revolutionary parties are important enough in their respective spheres, but they cannot always be accepted even as indicating the direction of the social current. The arbitrary acts of the most powerful ruler can avail little against the solid and massive sweep of great historic movements. Compared with the potent forces embodied and set in motion by the printing-press and the steam-engine, the achievements of the subtlest politicians and the greatest conquerors are vanity and idleness.

Such a contention is substantially true. History is a development of real forces, compared with which the doings of the noisiest and most prominent men are often only as the bubbles that rise and disappear on the top of the waves. Let us not, however, make any mistake as to what these real forces are. History narrates the movement of the great human society, and society is a most complex thing, in which we must recognise the operation of the most catholic variety of forces, technical, industrial, political, and moral. But the active and decisive elements in the whole process are the will and intelligence of men. Social forces are the many-sided expression of the will and intelligence of men acting on their environment, phases of the common activity of man adapting to his needs the resources of nature. The laws which regulate social development are the laws of the joint action of man on nature. What we have chiefly to study in social evolution are the laws of the development of human character.

In the study of the social movement, therefore, discussion as to the possibilities of human nature has its value. Our great difficulty is that we so little know how a complex mass of human beings will act under new conditions. Moreover, the doings of individual men may be of supreme importance, provided they are favoured by great historic tendencies. When the fulness of the time has come, the individual, whether he be autocrat, statesman, or popular leader, may most powerfully contribute towards the making of history. The likings and aspirations of men are, indeed, circumscribed by fixed natural conditions, but they are potent enough when organised into a vast force like the modern democracy. The democracy is the greatest power of modern times, and it is only an abstract name for the people educated and organised for the assertion of their political and economic rights. It is only a general name for the human beings most directly concerned in the social movement, with their wide diversity of capacity, interests, and aspirations.

In human society, as in everything else, we see a continual process of change going on. When the process of change grows rapid, intense, or contradictory, when the forces that make for change fall into conflict, or lead to an abrupt and sudden alteration in the course of development, we call it a revolution. A revolution is merely an abrupt or violent form of evolution. The order of the world is being continually renewed. The new is continually issuing out of the old. Centuries may elapse before an era runs its course, yet the change goes on from day to day. When a new time is born the seeds of decay are born with it, and they gradually develop with it, though the date of their large and visible operation may be far off. But with the decay of the old the formation of another order begins, so that the process of development is incessant. Thus the tendency towards transformation in society is made up of two phases, which it is not always easy to distinguish—of dissolution and reconstruction—which go on simultaneously. Before the old order is broken up—in the very process of breaking up—a new order is produced.

The name of revolution is generally applied to the rapid, abrupt, or violent transformations which signalise the breaking up of an old historic order. In the development of society there are successive epochs, marked by characteristic features, economic, social, and religious, more or less suited to each other. But a time comes in the progress of mankind when these become antiquated, useless, superfluous, and finally hurtful. The institutions and social forms which in one century are the progressive and even adequate expression of the life of the people may in the next century become an obstacle to progress. Thus the ideal of one period is the real of the next, and in the third probably is an abuse and a hindrance to further improvement. The new opinion is at first suspected, misrepresented, and condemned, and its adherents are boycotted, imprisoned, banished, or put to death. By and by it wins its way till it takes its place in the established order of things, or it is itself a new order of things. Once established, it becomes the centre and consolidating point of all human feelings and concerns—sentiments of loyalty and reverence, selfish interests, and generally of all that inertia which disposes men to accept things as they are, so long as they are fairly tolerable. But there are always forward and inquiring intellects on the quest for things new; and the mere progress of events disturbs that adaptation of institutions to the needs of the time which was once so satisfying. Innovating and even revolutionary ideas gradually gather head against established interests and the inertia of a settled society. If wise, timely, and energetic reform does not intervene to enforce a working compromise between old and new, a revolution is possible. In any case the old order cannot indefinitely survive. The process of change therefore must go forward, yet it is obviously better when the progress of the world can be secured without the catastrophe called a revolution. The most durable and beneficent progress is that of wise, gradual, and energetic adaptation of our institutions to the needs of the time. It is one of the exaggerations of many recent and contemporary socialists that they insist too much on the function and value of revolutions in the development of society.

Thus, in the evolution of society, the continuity is preserved through an incessant process of change, which is generally gradual, but sometimes becomes rapid and even violent, breaking out in sudden catastrophes and great cataclysms. But whether the change be sudden or gradual, whether it be a slow and steady progress through a settled epoch or the abrupt transition from an old into a new order of things, it must be in harmony with law. In accordance with this, the only correct view of the matter, the beginnings of great changes can be observed long before their actual realisation. Centuries before a great historic change makes its real and substantial—its large and visible—entrance in the affairs of the world the seeds of the coming time are sown, the conditions necessary for its growth are established. Its progress may be at one point promoted, and at another retarded, by a variety of causes, yet it ever advances towards the fulfilment of its time. The eye that is open to the facts can even form to itself some kind of forecast of the approaching era. It may only be a conjecture, but if the observer have any real gift of insight he may have a vision, and not an altogether false or obscure one, of the coming time. Thus, in the study of social phenomena, insight is foresight. The main condition of success is that we have our eyes open to the facts of the time in which we live. The chief reason why great changes take men by surprise is that they are engrossed with the pedantries of the past or are absorbed in some narrow interest of the present, while the great movement goes forward beyond the range of their spiritual vision. Indeed, it requires no particular sagacity to see the signs of a great historic change, provided we keep our eyes open, and are humble enough to learn and to submit our understanding to the objective truth of things. The religious revolt of the sixteenth century was announced long before it came. The revolution of the eighteenth was spreading all over Europe before it exploded at Paris in 1789. At the present time every country of the civilised world shows symptoms that the new democracy is in action. Every daily newspaper speaks of it; and while the details are of the most unexpected and incalculable nature, the general direction of the movement is apparent enough to all who are ready to see.

Now, socialism claims to be the next stage in social evolution. Under the conditions which prevail or tend to prevail in the development of society, it professes to be the fittest type of economic structure; it claims to be that form of industry which is fittest to carry on the progress of the world. In accordance with what we have been saying, if there is any foundation for such a claim, the tendencies which make for socialism must be already visible. Forces strong enough to establish it as a new social order must be already in action. Great changes do not come by magic, but are a slow growth out of facts and conditions already existing. In the existing society do we see any symptoms of that double process of dissolution and reconstruction which mark the rise of a new order of things, and do these symptoms point towards socialism?

We shall now, therefore, proceed to discuss those symptoms and tendencies in the existing society which may be supposed to make for socialism.

Tendencies towards Socialism

1. It is no exaggeration to say that the prevailing system of individualism shows clear signs of breaking down. We have already discussed the shortcomings of the competitive order of society, and we need here only review a few of the leading points. As we have seen, the general theory of this system is that human interests can be best promoted by each man attending

to his own. Considered as a system of industry and of government it cannot bear examination in point of principle, and experience has found it wanting. No sooner had the free struggle of individual energy and self-interest succeeded in breaking the bonds of the past than the necessity of new restrictions for the protection of human beings threatened with moral and physical ruin by the excesses of the new industrialism became apparent. The theory of *laissez-faire* broke down in all directions ; and the enormities of private selfishness had to be controlled by a multitude of public enactments, such as Factory Acts. As a theory of economics and of industry, individualism is now either given up or held with such a variety of limitations and qualifications as largely to deprive it of force and meaning. It is the theory of a generation that is passing away, and, as with all old theories, we are beginning to wonder how reasonable men could entertain it at all.

The present economic order must be condemned because involving a new form of subjection inconsistent with a free and educated democracy, and because tending to a competitive anarchy hurtful to all classes ; in short, it is inconsistent with the prevailing moral and political ideas and convictions of our time. It is adverse to order and security, to a real and durable freedom, and to the true moral development of men. But for the action of many countervailing influences the real nature and tendency of the competitive system would have been much sooner and much more clearly revealed. The principle of *laissez-faire* is sound and good so far, but it is only part of the truth. The time has come when it should take its place as an item in a wider and more comprehensive body of truth.

2. As we have seen, one of the first symptoms of the industrial revolution was the organisation and concentration of production in large factories, with an improved mechanical power and a large number of wage labourers. The small industry of the cottage weaver and of the village artisan, working with their own capital, was in this way superseded. This process of concentration still continues, more and more affecting every department of industry and attaining to ever larger dimensions. It is a patent fact, which marks the advance of capitalism and of the new industrialism all over the world. The process is an inevitable one, for with his inferior appliances and his imperfect organisation the small capitalist cannot hold his own against his larger rival. The margin of profit is now so extremely small that it is only from operations conducted on an enormous scale that a sufficient remuneration can be obtained. Even the large capitalist is giving place to the company; a growing proportion of business can be managed only by gigantic companies with an immense capital, an elaborate organisation, and an army of work-people. Success depends most of all on skilful, energetic organisation, and on the magnitude and efficiency of the industrial mechanism. In keeping with the general expansion the market also widens, until it embraces entire countries and the whole world; and in this world-market it is only the most powerful competitor, fighting with enormous capital and with the best natural advantages, that has any chance of prosperity or even of self-preservation.

Obviously this vast process of concentration cannot be brought about without creating disturbance and confusion over wide areas, involving in ruin thousands of luckless competitors. The variations of fortune, the alternations of success, are many; but it is the largest, the most energetic, the best organised competitor, working with the best natural resources, that emerges triumphant. Success leads to an enlarged business, and enlarged business on the whole leads to greater efficiency in the competitive struggle.

One of the most conspicuous signs of this process at the present day is the frequent transformation of private firms into limited liability companies. As businesses increase, the cares and responsibilities of ownership and management become too great for any single man. The further tendency towards the fusion or combination of companies is in various forms and under various names observable in Germany, Great Britain, and other countries.

But the most notable examples of the enormous scale on which business is now conducted must be found in the great industrial corporations of America. These companies control the production and exchange of a continent, and they show a capacity for the combination of interests and for fighting each other which we have not attained in this country. Combination in order to ruin their competitors, so as to secure an effective monopoly of the market—this is the aim and tendency of the great industrial struggle, carried out with an energy and on a scale elsewhere unexampled. The result is to put economic power in the hands of the combined corporations, to place at their mercy the sources and means of subsistence of the people, and from this point of vantage to gain control of American society generally—to establish an industrial oligarchy such as the world has never seen.

Hitherto we have witnessed the struggle of the democracy with the territorial aristocracy ; in America, as elsewhere, we now see the opening stages of a greater struggle, of the democracy against the industrial corporations, against the industrial feudal power, the fully developed capitalism. Either it must control the American people or the American people must control it. The issue must either be a new industrial oligarchy served by wage-labour, or the control of American industry for the good of the people.

At any rate, socialists regard these colossal corporations and the wealthy capitalists that direct them as the greatest pioneers of their cause. By concentrating the economic functions of the country into large masses they are simply helping forward the socialistic movement. Their mission is to displace the smaller capitalists, but they will thereby eventually undermine capitalism altogether. In proportion as the centralisation of industry is pushed forward, the easier will it be for the democratic people to displace its capitalistic chiefs, and assume the control of it for the general good. They are only hastening the time when a vast educated and organised democracy, subsisting on precarious wage-labour, will find itself face to face with a limited number of mammoth capitalists. Such a crisis can have only one result. The swifter, the more complete the success of the most powerful organisers of capital, the quicker will be their overthrow by a democratic society. Such is the belief of socialists.

The future course of the struggle is uncertain. Its normal development to the present time is apparent enough. The general march of social evolution has been, displacement of the small village or rural producer by the individual capitalist, transformation of the individual capitalist into the company, and now the company itself is being merged into the trust or combination of companies. It has been a continual process of expansion and centralisation, which now tends to monopoly. And this tendency to monopoly is only another proof that the system of free competition is inadequate and has broken down.

It should also be sufficiently clear that under the prevailing conditions of concentration and centralisation individual industry has not only ceased to be the normal and prevalent form, but tends more and more to disappear. Industry tends more and more to be a large operation conducted by the collective labour of many men and women. It is a social operation depending on the combined and organised exertion of thousands of workers. In fact, it depends on the useful work and service of the entire society, and it is impossible to discriminate the part performed in it by any single individual. In the earlier stages of the industrial revolution the capitalist was often originally a workman, and he continued effectively to initiate and manage the entire business in all its branches. He made his way, by superior energy, sagacity, and industry, to the head of a large establishment. It is very different now. With him still rest the ownership of the capital and the appropriation of the results of industry; but the actual work is done by thousands of toilers, all of them rendering their special services, and contributing a quota of their own to the collective product. Industry is no longer an individual function, as on the whole it was under the old and more primitive systems. Individual property and individual appropriation of the fruits of industry rigorously continue, but individual industry is growing to be a thing of the past. Industry is a social operation, a function of society, a collective process. The fact that industry has thus become social naturally suggests that distribution should be social and equitable.

3. In connection with the continual aggregation of business in large companies there is an important point which is worthy of special consideration. In proportion as these companies grow, the active and effective management must be intrusted to paid officials, and the capitalist ceases to be the real controller of industry; he tends to become a receiver of interest and dividends. Consequently the class which has hitherto been the ruling and governing one in the present economic order tends to become inactive and superfluous. In the inevitable process of industrial evolution it is being divested of the real and positive responsibilities connected with the industrial control of society. This transference of actual work and responsibility to manager and secretary with a large staff of clerks is by no means complete or general, but it is rapidly going forward.

In the evolution of modern society we can see a remarkable development of superfluous functionaries. Royalty, which both in feudal and more recent times was the active and effective head of the state, is, if not abolished, a mere survival in most countries of

Europe. Bismarck was the real founder and ruler of the new Germany, and he had to reckon with the people. The influence exerted by the present Emperor is a very exceptional thing. How long will the Autocrat of All the Russias retain his position against the growing revolutionary opinion among his people? In England the real ruler is the Prime Minister for the time being. He is placed in that position by the vote of the collective society; to it he must make appeal, and to it he must give account of his stewardship. As the nominal head of England the sovereign fills his anomalous post with tact, discretion, and dignity; but his effective power is extremely limited.

In former times the landholding aristocracy formed a power second only to that of the monarch; often, indeed, co-ordinate with it, and even controlling it. In feudal times they performed the military and many of the judicial functions. After the revolution of 1689 they practically ruled England for several generations, constituting the House of Lords and nominating the majority of the House of Commons; and they controlled local government still more effectually. Now they have greatly lost influence in the Commons, and in real power the Lords hold quite an inferior position. The effect of the reform of local government will be still further to supersede the aristocracy—in the various districts to establish the rule of society or the community in place of the old rule by the landowners. The whole tendency of our social evolution is to supersede the old rule of Crown and aristocracy, and to set up in its stead a government by the chosen leaders of the collective society. The will of the whole society with its elected chiefs asserts itself against hereditary rulers representing narrow and exclusive interests.

The active heads of the present industrial order are the capitalists ; but we have seen that as the large industry develops into great companies the effective management passes into the hands of paid officials. It is obvious how the development of such a tendency could facilitate the transference of the great industries to social control. For example, with regard to the railway system of England, if it should appear expedient to place it under collective management, the state would find a staff of officials and *employés* ready to its hand. The present organisation, modified chiefly in the direction of further centralisation and greater economy, would be sufficient. As society is displacing royalty and the landholding aristocracy, so will it displace the capitalist rulers of the great industrial companies.

4. The decisive fact in the social development of modern times is the growth of the democracy. The first great phase of it was the rise of the middle classes, dating in a general way from the French Revolution of 1789. Behind the middle classes, however, have emerged the workmen, whose consolidation as a special class began with the revolutionary periods of 1830 and 1848. While the democracy in its widest sense is simply a government by the people generally in their own interests, the working class may be regarded as the representatives of the democracy in the narrower sense. But as they form the immense majority of the people in every country, it is the entrance of the

labouring class on the political stage which has led to the formation of a real democracy.

The rise of the middle class against the old aristocracies was an important fact, but the awakening of the labouring people is an event vastly more momentous. The workers at the loom, miners, the cultivators of the soil, the toilers of the sea, all these have arisen out of the bondage and darkness wherein they have been sunk from time immemorial, to claim their share in the heritage of light and happiness. Surely their claim is a just and right one, the most righteous and the most momentous ever made by human beings since the birth of time.

This democracy, as we are all aware, is being formed and moulded under a set of conditions which are a new thing in the history of the world. Since 1848 it has received political power, and it has begun to pass through the elementary school in all lands. Besides being drilled into industrial armies in the large factory and railway system, it forms the vast national armies of the new military system. In a word, the school, the press, the new industrial system, and the new military system have all combined to instruct and organise the modern democracy, and thus to create a colossal force, which has already begun to take a considerable part in the affairs of men. In the gigantic electoral contests which continually recur in every civilised country, in the great labour struggles which never cease, this democracy is learning to know its strength. A long and hard experience is impressing upon it a sense of community of interest. It is consolidating into a class. Further, it must be said that in many lands the leaders of the democracy have been serving a severe and stern apprenticeship of suffering in secret conspiracy, in unsuccessful revolt, in prison and exile, and on the scaffold. Though we regard it not, such a course of training will some day have results of which we may hear. A cause for which men will die is a serious one. It is a discipline which great causes, capable of a mighty future and potent in moulding the destinies of men, have generally had to undergo.

But the most important fact in connection with the democracies is that while they are nominally, and might be really, the supreme possessors of political power, they are economically a mass of proletarians. This contrast between their political and economical position is the most significant feature of our time, and supplies the key to most of the questions now pending. For the most part the difficulties of our time are only the expression of the discontent of the democracy with its economic position. Scarcely a newspaper but records some incident in the struggle of the democracy to better itself. Agrarian troubles in Ireland and elsewhere, strikes in the industrial centres, riots, demonstrations of unemployed and discontented workmen, special legislation for the common people forced upon reluctant parliaments of landholders and capitalists—all these have been symptoms of the rise of a new class to a position of power. In one form or other these symptoms have been declaring themselves in every part of the civilised world.

Perhaps the most notable result of the industrial revolution is that it has supplied the technical conditions for a durable and progressive democracy; it has placed the modern democracy on a firm and solid basis. Society is now based on a vast mechanism, of which the motive powers are steam and electricity. The application of steam to printing has furnished us with all the appliances of education, so that universal education is an accomplished fact. It has given us the cheap newspaper and provided us with cheap literature, bringing within the reach of every citizen facilities for reading and culture. Through the combined agency of the telegraph and the printing-press the speeches and utterances of our leading statesmen and other guides of public opinion can be read by every one, almost as soon as they are delivered. The constant outpouring of cultivated and uncultivated reflection in the press and on the platform has its drawbacks, but it at least acts as a continual stimulus to the intelligence of the people. The successive facts of public life and of the history of the world as presented in the press supply a constant process of education and cultivation to the whole body of citizens. The mass of the people share in an intellectual movement which was formerly confined to a few. Knowledge and culture are no longer the monopoly of a privileged minority. The democratic culture may not have the refinement and distinction characteristic of an exclusive and aristocratic society, but the whole movement will secure a vastly higher moral and intellectual life for the masses of the people.

From these considerations it will be obvious that the democracy is not an accident dependent merely on the acceptance of a novel set of opinions fitted to have a temporary vogue, but the solid result of the strongest forces of our time. It is the outcome of our entire technical, industrial, social, and political development, the effect of massive causes, which are operating in every civilised country. It is growing to be the master-force of the world; and as the years proceed its influence will more and more develop itself.

5. The growth of state and municipal socialism is simply a phase of the development of the democracy. It is unnecessary here to enlarge upon the fact that in the past the state has been the organ of a narrow class. It is only since 1832 that in this country it has really begun to represent the masses of the people. Even yet the effective representation of the lower middle class and of the working classes in the Government is very slight. The possession of considerable means is still almost essential for becoming a member of Parliament. We have not yet an effective democracy. But it is growing, and as compared with the slow progress of the past it is growing rapidly.

It is a remarkable fact that the most eminent examples of state socialism are to be found in countries so different as Germany and New Zealand. The menacing growth of social democracy in Germany led not only to repressive legislation, but also to positive and remedial measures of insurance for working men against accident, sickness, and old age. From 1881, when these measures were announced, till the end of 1903 the sums spent on insurance against illness amounted to 100,000,000*l*., on insurance against accidents to 45,000,000*l*., and on old-age pensions to 42,500,000*l*. The persons who benefited by the measures numbered 60,000,000. Under the direct inspiration of the democracy in New Zealand state socialism has taken the form of banking, land legislation, compulsory arbitration, and old-age pensions of 10*s*. a week for persons over sixty-five years of age. Similar legislation of a notable character is at work in Denmark and Australia.

These, however, are only the most conspicuous instances of a tendency which is visible and is more or less rapidly growing over the world. In all countries which have any claim to be called enlightened or progressive, the duty and necessity of social legislation are being pressed on Governments whether they be willing or reluctant. The conditions under which rulers live and work are undergoing a change: the atmosphere is new.

In municipal socialism we see the growth of a like tendency. The reform of our municipal government in 1835 was a popular measure, which has had a most beneficial influence. Experience has proved that such local rule may with advantage be extended in many directions. Lighting, water, tramways, parks and means of recreation, better housing for the poor, the interests of public health, and to a large degree education, are all now regarded as belonging to the legitimate sphere of local government. By-and-by we may see local control effectively extended to building sites and the drink question. It is now the veriest truism to maintain that the popular interests, and especially the interests of the suffering classes, should be promoted through the common action of local centres by all wise and effectual methods. Controversy is still very acute as to how far it may be carried, but there can be no dispute about the general principle.

The development of state and municipal socialism is due to the pressure of the democracy on our rulers and on the existing institutions; and it is likely to extend more and more as the people attain to a clearer consciousness of their rights and to a more effectual organisation.

6. We have already spoken of the solid tendency towards a new social order observable in the inevitable concentration and centralisation of industry. There have, however, been more conscious efforts towards a new order, which, though only partial and incomplete, clearly prove that society cannot exist on negations, but must require a real and positive satisfaction of its needs. As soon as this country had recovered its freedom and elasticity after the conclusion of the great wars with Napoleon, as soon as our antiquated and reactionary government had begun to relax, a new period of social growth set in. One of the first signs of new life was the rise of societies and associations of every kind. They were a sufficient proof that the prevalent individualism was only part of the truth; that there was a larger and far more important element of the truth in the principle that the individual must seek to realise himself in union with his fellow-men, and that the new time and the new circumstances required new forms of associated life. It was a spontaneous development of social life seeking new methods of satisfying real and natural needs.

In the industrial sphere we have had many of these efforts towards a new social order. Factory Acts imposed on the capitalists by Government on grounds of public necessity and in opposition to the prevailing economic theory, trade unions, the co-operative system, the industrial partnership system, boards of conciliation, even employers' combinations, may all be regarded as a real and effective preparation for a new organisation of industry. They may all be described as partial efforts to limit the violence of competition, to introduce a measure of system and regularity in industrial life, and in some degree at least to establish a new harmony and stability of interests. The doctrine of *laissez-faire* was useful in clearing the way for such a reconstruction. If Government could not rationally control industry except in matters so imperative as Factory Acts, it could at least leave industry free room to organise itself. When unreasonable and oppressive restrictions are removed, the development of popular life can take a natural course, and those efforts of which we have spoken indicate clearly enough the natural course of social development. Evidently what is needed is to carry on the work to its just and reasonable issue, and by free discussion and steady progress along well-tested lines to find our way to a better, a solid and stable society.

It may, indeed, be maintained that our competitive individualism is not an organic epoch at all, but is merely the negative and transitional state of things which marks the break-up of an old order and the preparation and imperfect realisation of a new.

As illustrating the growth of new social forms, the following statement of Mr. Ludlow, formerly Chief Registrar of Friendly Societies, has a special importance :—'Since I have been at this office I have been compelled to look at the different forms of societies in their mutual relations, and see that the friendly society is the common stock out of which all have sprung, and without which, for instance, neither co-operation nor trade unionism can really be understood. Spreading throughout the length and breadth of the country, to every trade and occupation, the humdrum friendly society has been *the* school of social self-government for our working class. It has not only supplied the machinery in the first instance for the building society, the co-operative society, the trade union; it has supplied the free spirit and the tendency to federation. France and Germany supply instances of the same influence differently exerted.'[1] Nothing can more clearly bring out the fact that the development of social forms since 1830 has arisen out of the elementary needs of human life; and it is to be hoped that they are only the imperfect beginnings of a new order resting on a broad and positive basis, and fitted to secure the highest ends of social union.

We have already indicated our belief that the most hopeful of all these forms of united effort is the co-operative movement. From about 1820 to 1845 there was a rapid multiplication of co-operative societies under the auspices of Robert Owen and his school. Most of these died out after a brief existence. The success of co-operation dates from the foundation of the Rochdale Pioneers in 1844. That society began in the humblest way. Twenty-eight poor weavers in hard times managed by subscriptions of twopence and threepence a week to raise a capital of twenty-eight pounds in order to open a store and supply themselves and their families with cheap and wholesome food. They adopted methods which could work, and they succeeded; and their society became a model and an encouragement to working men in other towns. At the end of twenty years the growth of the co-operative

[1] See *Manual for Co-operators*, p. 224.

societies, though moderate, had been such as to excite the admiration of men like W. E. Gladstone and J. S. Mill. In 1906 there were 1,588 societies with a membership of 2,332,000, a capital of 30,000,000*l*., an annual turnover of 98,000,000*l*., and an annual profit of 11,000,000*l*. English co-operation has been most successful in distribution. But the important matter is that with distribution as a basis, and by means of the capital and experience therein acquired, the societies are successfully and on a very considerable scale taking up the business of production. They have bakeries, corn mills, boot and other factories on a large scale. They have two wholesale societies in Manchester and Glasgow, doing an immense business in such production, as well as in wholesale distribution, with steamers of their own for the conveyance of goods from the Continent. Obviously the next step is to extend the co-operative system to farming—a way of deliverance for English farming will probably be found in this direction. At any rate the success of co-operation in the past gives encouragement for the widest application of its methods to industry. The gist of the movement is that the workmen, by means of a joint capital, equitably manage their own economic interests. In England it began with distribution, and now proceeds to occupy the other departments of industry.

In Germany and Italy co-operation has flourished most as applied to people's banks; but there, as in England, it is occupying other fields also. The German movement began in 1849 on the most insignificant scale. We cannot here give the history of the movement. At the beginning of 1885, there were in connection with the Schulze-Delitzsch system 3,822 co-operative societies, of which there were 1,965 loan and credit societies, 678 co-operative store societies, 1,146 of a miscellaneous character, and 33 building societies. The number of members was 1,500,000 with 15,000,000*l*. of their own capital and 25,000,000*l*. of borrowed capital. Their annual business amounted to 150,000,000*l*.

Co-operation is making notable progress in Belgium. The town of Ghent has been its chief centre, and in Ghent the most notable pioneer of the movement is the Vooruit Society. It is doing for Belgium what the Rochdale Pioneers have done for co-operation in England, but in a far more revolutionary way, for the Vooruit is avowedly but a means to promote the realisation of the programme of the Socialist party in Belgium. The Vooruit was founded by E. Anseele and a few poor weavers at a time of scarcity in 1873. Their capital at first was about 3*l*. 8*s*., with which they started a bakery. From this very small beginning the society has gone on to establish huge stores, the largest cotton factory in Ghent with an eight hours' day, printing works, a daily and weekly press, a system of life insurance and of old-age pensions. It also offers the means of education and recreation at its People's Palace. It is estimated that out of a population of 165,000 in Ghent the social economic life of 100,000 depends on the Vooruit. It has served as a model for similar institutions in Belgium, as also in Holland, Germany, and France. In Denmark, Ireland, France, South Africa, India and many other countries co-operation has been making rapid strides, particularly in agriculture. Statistics now seem unable to keep pace with it. Statesmen of all parties regard it as a beneficent power with a future before it which cannot be measured.

This very slight sketch is enough to show that the co-operative movement throughout the world is full of vitality, and of the widest and most far-reaching promise of usefulness. No one can deny that it is in theory superior to the present system, and it has shown its working fitness under very trying circumstances in many countries. Having proved that it is the fittest type of industry under the dominant conditions of the present time, it must survive and prevail. In the words of J. S. Mill, 'when, however, co-operative societies shall have sufficiently multiplied, it is not probable that any but the least valuable workpeople will any longer consent to work all their lives for wages merely; and both private capitalists and associations will gradually find it necessary to make the entire body of labourers participants in profits. Eventually, and in perhaps a less remote future than may be supposed, we may, through the co-operative principle, see our way to a change in society which would combine the freedom and independence of the individual with the moral, intellectual, and economical advantages of aggregate production; and which, without violence or spoliation, or even any sudden disturbance of existing habits and expectations, would realise, at least in the industrial department, the best aspirations of the democratic spirit by putting an end to the division of society into the industrious and the idle, and effacing all social distinctions but those fairly earned by personal services and exertions.' [1]

[1] *Political Economy*, People's Edition, 476.

Under the forementioned six heads, then, we have enumerated the tendencies which may be regarded as at present making for socialism, and which in any case will have a powerful influence on the social development of the future. The positive tendencies which we have pointed out are all phases of the concentration of industry on the one hand, and of the rise and consolidation of the democracy on the other. These two, it may be said, are the cardinal and decisive facts of our time—the industrial revolution and the rise of the democracy. And the two are most intimately connected with each other, both in principle and historical development.

The two together have produced the theory of economic and social life embodied in modern socialism, and through them the movement expects to be realised. Socialism depends for its realisation on the irresistible momentum of two great revolutions—the industrial revolution and the political revolution named the new democracy. It seeks to render the mechanism of the industrial revolution really subservient to human welfare, and to realise a social and economic freedom suited to the political freedom proclaimed in the modern democracy. It is in the centralisation of industrial processes that socialism finds its economic basis. Like the democracy, socialism aims at the realisation of freedom for the mass of mankind; not the negative freedom of *laissez-faire*, but a substantial, well-ordered freedom; not the one-sided and delusive freedom of individualism, but one that has regard to the economic and social needs of man; freedom under moral and economic conditions suited to the fuller and more harmonious development of human beings;

freedom wedded to moral law, to art and knowledge.

Thus it does appear to be one of the strongest points of socialism that it proposes a free organisation of industry, which may serve as economic complement to that political freedom which is the ideal of the democracy. The theory of the democracy is that the people obey laws of their own making, that they choose their own servants, and conduct government for their own good. The government favoured by the democracy is self-government in their own interest. In the economic sphere we want a corresponding form of self-governing industry, a free industrial democracy. Socialism claims to be industry of the people, by the people, for the people.

In our review we see tendency rising into a clear and deliberate purpose. Socialism and democracy appear to be forming a conscious union as social democracy; but both are changed in the process. We cannot too strongly insist that socialism is not a stereotyped system of dogma. In the democracy we see abundant life and incessant change. Since modern freedom began with the granting of Magna Charta and the founding of the House of Commons in the thirteenth century, men have been feeling their way to a better society. Every century since that time has seen successes chequered by disastrous failures. How well we now know that freedom has its risks and responsibilities as well as its blessings! From 1789, when the democracy made its great entry on the world's stage, the history of France and of Europe has been an impressive illustration of the momentous truth that great changes in human affairs cannot rightly be forced or improvised. They can be well and duly made only when the minds and hearts of men are prepared for them. Force is useful, and even necessary sometimes, to sweep away old forms of abuse ; but it is otherwise of little avail. Marx said a true word when he wrote that ‘ the working class cannot simply take possession of the ready State machine, and set it in motion for its own purposes.’

But the successes of the democracy are ever becoming more frequent, the flowing tide is with it. In order to shape the vague tendencies of evolution into a better society it needs wisdom and nobler ideals. A rich and varied experience won by painful effort and at a terrible cost is already available. This experience is accumulating every year. The progressive countries of the world now form a vast social laboratory in which experiments are continually being made for the common benefit of mankind. Even such as have been most backward can now offer a valuable lesson to the rest. England, France, Germany, Denmark, and Italy have shown the way to the world ; and now Belgium may claim the foremost place. The latest phase of democracy is in some respects the most encouraging of all. At the General Election in Austria in 1907, the first held on the basis of universal suffrage, the democracy gave promise that it will be a real bond of union to a country long distracted by racial animosity. If it succeed in bringing some degree of peace and brotherhood to the valley of the Danube, which, since the dawn of history, has been devastated and drenched with blood, there is not a task in the world which it may not cheerfully undertake.

CHAPTER IX

CONCLUSION

We have now come to the summing up of our subject. And first as to the problem which socialism has undertaken to solve. As we have seen, the worker was set free on the downfall of Feudalism; but his emancipation was accompanied or followed by his divorce from the soil. The classes that had possession of the land held also the reins of government, local and national; and the English labourer was in time reduced to a new form of service, under which his wages were regulated by those who were interested in keeping them low, his personal freedom limited by laws of settlement, his mind kept in ignorance, and scope for development almost wholly denied him. When the industrial revolution came, the men who owned the capital and directed industry also gained political power. Under the new régime, as under the old, the workers lost control of the means of subsistence, and suffered all manner of social and political disability.

In America the struggle for wealth has led to the rise of the great corporations, which possess a more or less effective monopoly of industry and commerce. This struggle, it should be noted, has been fought under the most favourable conditions by representatives of the strongest races in the world in accordance with their most deeply cherished ideals. That is to say, it is the freest individual struggle for success among champions fairly matched that has thus resulted in monopoly. If history teaches anything clearly, it teaches that in the long run social and political power goes with the economic and industrial. From the vantage ground of the possession of the means of subsistence and culture an oligarchy thus established under such extraordinary conditions will, if unchecked, control the destinies of the American people. If unchecked it will control not only industry and commerce, but legislation, administration, and the press. Art, literature and science, churches and universities will look to the plutocracy for support. Once established, the oligarchy will, like the dominant forms of government in the Old World, receive the sanction of custom and tradition, from which ordinary minds have so much difficulty in emancipating themselves. The divine right of success so imposing and so dear to the average sensual man will take the place of the divine right of kings, and round it will gather all the sentiments and sanctions that go with possession, prescription, political power, and the ascendancy of wealth. To some degree the oligarchy may be expected to establish an order unattainable under free competition. But only to some degree, for we may expect also to see the fiercest and wildest struggles in its own midst, in the frenzied speculation of Wall Street, in the great contests for political influence, and in other forms. Here we have a power which is a menace to all that Americans have held dear. And here we have, in its most formidable form, the problem which socialism has undertaken to solve.

We may expect that the supervision and control of the trusts by the State will be beneficial as far as it goes. But who can guarantee that in the future the executive will not itself be nominated and controlled by the trusts? It is impossible to exaggerate the gravity of the position.

America, however, merely offers us the latest, the most gigantic, and the most impressive example of a movement which is observable in nearly every part of the world. We can for some centuries trace the development of its historical forms in our own country. But the origin and motive of the movement must be found in human nature itself.

Every phase of the movement is coloured by human nature. But it is the most serious objection to the prevalent competitive system that it has given scope, incitement—and also to a large degree justification—for many of the worst and vilest human passions. At one time it could fairly claim to be a stage in the development of human freedom. It could with more reason insist that it led to a notable increase in the energy and efficiency of the productive forces. There were moral qualities of diligence, forethought, sobriety, and self-control which it could reasonably maintain to have fostered. But we have now reached a higher point of view from which we can see that it is no longer a help, but a serious hindrance to the economic, political, and moral development of the human race. The chief task of the truly enlightened mind now is to find a fitting type for the progressive evolution of the future. The fact that the evils of competition are making way for the evils of monopoly only renders the task more urgent.

The claim of socialism to hold the field as a fitting system for the progressive evolution of the future becomes more urgent as time goes on. We have already tried to explain what the socialistic solution of the problem is. But it may be well once more, clearly and emphatically, to dissociate it from theories which have produced so much confusion and misunderstanding. Socialism has no necessary connection with materialism or with theories subversive of religion, marriage, and the family. The abstract and rigid collectivism which figures in so many socialistic programmes is not consistent with a reasonable view of the subject. Surplus value and other abstract theories of Marx do not belong to the essence of the subject. The regimental or bureaucratic socialism which seems to be favoured by some writers, is absolutely alien to any reasonable conception of socialism. Pedantry and dogmatism in any form do not accord with the genuine socialistic spirit, which above all things demands the seeing eye and the open mind. Readiness to learn both from discussion and experience, the freest spirit of inquiry should be the characteristics of all socialists.

Socialism is a new type of economic organisation. It means that industry should be carried on by associated workers, using a joint capital with a view to an equitable system of distribution. This economic organisation is naturally correlated to democracy in politics and to altruism in ethics. As I have said in my 'History of Socialism' (p. 381), 'Socialism rests on the great ideals of freedom and justice, of brotherhood and mutual service. It may well claim to be the heir of the great ideals of the greatest races. The

Hebrew ideal of truth, righteousness, and mercy which on its ethical side was widened and deepened into the Christian ideals of love, brotherhood, and mutual service, and the Greek ideal of the true, the good, and the beautiful all may and should be accepted by socialism, and they should be supplemented by the Roman conceptions of law, order, and continuity, but with far wider aims and meanings. In its law of mutual service, by which it at once asserted the interdependence of the members of the social organism and a profound conception of social duty, Christianity went deeper both in philosophy and practice than the French Revolution with its watchwords of liberty, equality, and fraternity.' It is the crowning function of socialism that it offers new economic forms for the moral, social, and political development of mankind. In the past we have had the rule of classes and nations leading to the subjection of the weak. It was believed that freedom with competition would do away with subjection. But it has been found that the competitive struggle only leads to new forms of mastery for the few and subjection for the many. Class rule and competition must alike give place to a freedom which can be won and secured only by association on a solid economic basis. The free development of men must go hand in hand with association.

From the point of view of socialism the State must be regarded as an association for the promotion of the good of all its members, so far as it can be furthered by the central organ. The municipality or commune must, from the same point of view, be regarded as an organ for the promotion of the good of the people so far as it can be furthered locally. The co-operative society should be regarded as an example of the new forms of association that may proceed out of the free initiative of the people.

Socialism may simply be regarded as a new and better conception of a very old principle or institution. It will insist on a better, a transformed State. Its conception is really that of Aristotle, elevated, deepened and widened in accordance with the many-sided and far-reaching ideal which we have set forth. We must make the natural and real a basis for the attaining of the ideal. But the State, as we have it in England and other countries, falls lamentably short of any reasonable ideal. We have a large and highly organised public service. The Church, army and navy, justice and police, schools and universities, the postal and telegraph services, are all public functions; and posts in every one of these departments are eagerly competed for, from the office of Prime Minister downwards. What we should now see is that many of the functions and activities of the State relating to court life and diplomacy, military affairs and finance, are not only superfluous and survivals of old times, but are highly pernicious. The State, with its wide functions and ample resources, should be organised to promote the welfare and the freedom of the whole community.

In regard to the municipality or commune, we should remember that it has had to rely almost entirely on the rates for the means to carry out its vast and much-needed tasks. Through the negligence and corruption of past times local bodies have been stripped of the common lands which should have been used to defray expenditure. Urban land should be municipal property. For the solution of the land question in the country the ideal to keep before our eyes is the homestead large enough to employ and support a family, and worked by co-operative methods. Land reform in town, village, and country is urgently needed to give scope for social progress. The homestead may or may not, but it probably should, be associated, as of old, with the village community. Occupation should be permanent under the sanction and furtherance of the community.

Of all great countries Germany has the most efficient political system, in which State, municipality and private enterprise combine for the promotion of common ends. The patriotic spirit has already led the nation a long way in the public ownership and use of public utilities, in State and municipal socialism. Even urban land is becoming urban property. But there is a great gulf fixed between the governing classes and the Social Democracy. While in many respects Great Britain is behind Germany, we have the supreme advantage of a freer system. We have it in our power above all other countries to secure the free common action of all the organs and members of the community. And we have had the supreme opportunity of showing for the first time in the history of the world how a great empire can be transformed into a free association of States. The ideal of socialism is the free service of society and the free exchange of mutual service among its members. This ideal should be, and is being, applied to the transformation of empire. The British Empire is, and evermore should be, a free association of States in which the active and practical bond of union should be the free interchange of services.

The State has still too much the character of a taxing and fighting machine ; the municipality is too much an engine for the exacting of rates from the poor who cannot provide daily bread and shelter for their children, and so far as they remain at this stage merely they have neither part nor lot in the socialistic ideal. Let us not deceive ourselves with vain hopes of the speedy and complete realisation of that ideal. Yet we can see the solid framework of a new society growing out of the old. Faith and enthusiasm, as well as integrity, perseverance, and tried business capacity, are working for it on a broad and firm basis of successful experience. Within the wide compass of this new society there will be scope, support, and encouragement for the individual and the family, for local institutions and the nation, for new forms of free association, and all the factors of progressive human evolution ; and it will be one of the great problems of the future wisely to adjust them for the good of man. But in the future as in the past, progress will above all things else depend on the soundness of family life and on the recognition of the rights and duties of motherhood.

Generally it will be the aim of socialism to develop and perfect for the service of man the mechanism of the industrial revolution, and so to carry forward to a higher plane the evolution of the human race. By order, prevision, and the prevention of waste both of force and raw material and of human effort, it must show itself superior in economy and efficiency to the competitive system, and on this ground alone worthy to supersede it. But its chief aim will be to surpass it immeasurably in the equity and mercy of its methods of distribution. Rightly understood, it will be a discipline for the unsteady and unruly, a guide and support to the weak. To men generally it will appear as a type of economic organisation that may take form in a thousand diverse ways, an ideal to be realised by wise and strenuous effort, a goal resplendent and ever visible, which men will ever strive to attain. But the type will be always changing; the ideal will always grow more exacting and will never be perfectly realised; the goal, as we approach it, will recede and rise higher.

The indispensable basis, as we have seen, is merely an enlightened self-interest. But the ardent and generous soul will always cherish a noble ideal and strive for the higher goal. On a wide and firm real basis to give free and effectual scope to the ideal—this is the aim of a reasonable socialism. How far individual initiative and how far collective action may go in their relation to each other is a question that must be fought out in detail.

To accomplish these great ends it must enlist on its side all who hunger and thirst after righteousness, all who are touched with pity for the poor and needy, all who have in their hearts the love of order, comeliness, and beauty. We may regard it partly as the misfortune, but largely also as the fault of socialists that the movement has so often been divorced from the moral and spiritual forces which have done so much to shape the history of mankind. Socialism most intimately and essentially belongs to these forces. It is part of the great stream of tendency that makes for truth, righteousness, and mercy, for peace and brotherhood, order and beauty. These are all of its household; it can help them and it can claim their help.

The generous and impartial student of the socialistic movement must judge all men and institutions according to their conformity to this ideal. For him parties and forces have no worth, except in so far as they realise it in thought and action. In a happier time, when the memory of old enmities and misunderstandings shall have grown dim, the men and women of a nobler and more catholic society will, we trust, place the wreath of laurel on the tombs of Robert Owen and Lord Shaftesbury, of the Emperor William I. and Bismarck, as well as of Lassalle and Karl Marx, of Cardinal Manning and General Booth, as well as of the poor weavers of Rochdale and Ghent, who made the co-operative movement live. And on the commemoration days of the future they will think gratefully of all who, having fought and died in the cause of the poor, sleep in graves that are nameless and forgotten, whether in frost-bound Siberia, under the burning sun of the tropics, or in the crowded cemeteries of our great cities.

The poet had a dream that 'Time will run back and fetch the Age of Gold.' We trust that Time will run *on* to fetch the Age of Gold. We may be of good hope that we shall see an era when men shall no longer 'grind the face of the poor.' 'And they shall beat their swords into plowshares, and their spears into pruning hooks; nation shall not lift up sword against nation, neither shall they learn war any more.'

THE END

Spottiswoode & Co. Ltd., Printers, New-street Square. London.